PLANTS ALIVE!

PLANTS ALIVE!

REVEALING PLANT LIVES THROUGH GUIDED NATURE JOURNALING

by
Charles E Roth
Foreword by Frank Knight

iUniverse, Inc.
New York   Lincoln   Shanghai

PLANTS ALIVE!
REVEALING PLANT LIVES THROUGH GUIDED NATURE JOURNALING

Copyright © 2005 by Charles E. Roth

iUniverse books may be ordered through booksellers or by contacting:

iUniverse
2021 Pine Lake Road, Suite 100
Lincoln, NE 68512
www.iuniverse.com
1-800-Authors (1-800-288-4677)

Illustrations

by
the author

and
Mary Sage Shakespeare

ISBN-13: 978-0-595-36644-6 (pbk)
ISBN-13: 978-0-595-82394-9 (cloth)
ISBN-13: 978-0-595-81066-6 (ebk)
ISBN-10: 0-595-36644-9 (pbk)
ISBN-10: 0-595-82394-7 (cloth)
ISBN-10: 0-595-81066-7 (ebk)

Printed in the United States of America

Contents

FOREWORD

The amount of time youngsters spend with television and video games currently commands a great deal of media attention. Obesity and a heightened tolerance for violence are among the decried outcomes. But when was the last time you heard any concern about the tube stealing children away from the joys of experiencing solitude while exploring a nearby fallow field or woodlot? There still are a few expressing concern that we are on the verge of losing our connections with nature; I would argue that we have already slipped over the edge. Nature appreciation is no longer a part of our popular culture.

Some would argue that that participating in outdoor activity is on the rise. Hiking and camping are popular ways to escape the stresses of life in our artificial world, but nature is little more than pleasing scenery. One wonders how much more satisfying these outdoor activities would be if folks could learn some natural history. There is likely much less hope for those who see nature as a bumpy blur while speeding through it on bikes, snowmobiles and ATVs.

Horticulturalist David Longland spoke of nature appreciation's role in shaping our personal development and social skills in his forward to Chuck Roth's earlier work, The Plant Observer's Guidebook (Prentice-Hall, 1984): "We derive an inner peace by revering our connectedness with our natural environment," and he quoted Sioux Chief Standing Bear: "Kinship with all creatures of the earth, sky and water was a real and active principle…The Indian knew that man's heart away from nature becomes hard; that lack of respect for living, growing things soon led to a lack of respect for humans too."

Of course, our understanding of plants and animals and their ecological relationships is also vital to our being effective environmental stewards. Governments are less likely to relax environmental standards and Creationists are less likely to diminish the theory of evolution in the face of an environmentally sophisticated citizenry.

So, how do we redirect attention from the scenery on the horizon to the wild geraniums at our feet? Chuck Roth's *Plants Alive!* is a worthy attempt to reach a variety of audiences. Gardeners firmly committed to the plants in their care will be drawn in by Chuck's encouragement to look beyond nurtured plants as treats for the palate or eye. His questions will have gardeners looking at life form, leaf arrangement, root structure and length of flowering time. A few will take that leap over the garden wall to compare garden plants with their wild relatives. Doing experiments and taking careful measurements and notes will not be for every reader, but the author's questioning format will stimulate curiosity and entice readers to think about possible answers.

For a variety of reasons, educators will embrace this book. First of all, it is a course in botany without any of the stigmas associated with textbooks. Also unlike texts, *Plants Alive!* enables students to do real science, and not just read about it. Experiments and exercises passed off as hands-on science abound, but opportunities for students to do real science and report their findings to the scientific community are rare.

Language arts teachers should be as enthusiastic as science teachers. Here, page after page, are topics to journal and hone creative writing skills. Combining science and writing lets teachers better educate the whole child through multi-disciplinary learning.

Chuck Roth asks a great deal of his readers. First, to answer questions that require carefully looking, measuring and timing. Then he would have you take the giant leap with commitment and discipline to journal your outdoor observations. He makes a compelling argument—moving from remembering vague emotions and moods to having detailed, retrievable records of what we experience on any given outing. Those who accept his challenge will be amply rewarded.

In the hands of a caring adult, *Plants Alive!* can help awaken youngsters to the wonders outdoors. Teachers and parents and grandparents need to take youngsters outside and share their enthusiasm for the wonders they find there. Give a child a journal and together record your fascinating finds. Today, fewer teachers have sufficient natural history knowledge to confidently take students outdoors. One solution is for those of us with an easy familiarity with the outdoors and its diversity to volunteer to work with schools and youth groups. What works best is how most of us became naturalists: guidance one on one with a caring enthusiastic adult!

Frank Knight
Naturalist-Photographer
Cohoes, NY

ACKNOWLEDGEMENTS

Although I have been a general naturalist all my life, my basic bent has been towards the animal world. It has taken a number of people over the years to help sharpen my knowledge and interest in the plant world. Probably my earliest botanical mentor was a savvy outdoorsman, amateur game manager and archaeologist, and an avid indoor and outdoor gardener, named **LeGrand "Sam" Stack.** From Sam I learned a lot of plant lore and gardening skills

I want to thank the many camps that I served as a nature counselor over the years for the opportunity they provided to learn about our native plants and their lore and to develop ways to pass some of this knowledge on to the many campers I came in contact with..

My first real professional involvement with botanical people came during my several years of serving as a weekend naturalist at the Greenwich Audubon Center where I came under the tutelage of master field botanist **Len Bradley** and my primary interpretive mentor **Charles Mohr.**

In college during the midl950's I had the great privilege of studying with Dr. **Wendell Camp** one of our premier explorers and field botanists and with Dr **Raymond Kienholz** of the wildlife biology program at the University of Connecticut. They broadened and deepened my understanding of the wonders of the plant world.

I also gained a great deal of botanical knowledge from Dr. **William Jahoda** and his friend Dr. **William Niering** of Connecticut College for Women.

I also treasure time I had with master botanical interpreter **May Thielgaard Watts** of the Morton Arboretum and with staff at the Taft Field Campus of the University of Northern Illinois who along with the **Aldo Leopold family** broadened my understanding of the prairie biomes which were quite foreign to a person brought up in the New England woodlands.

In terms of this particular book I would like to thank Bantam Books for permission to quote a number the people noted in their book <u>The Wisdom of the Elders</u> in my Guided Journaling Section.

I also thank Gibbs Smith for permission to quote from <u>Words From the Land</u> by Stephen Trimble.

I am also grateful to the John Burroughs Association for permission to quote the sage's words from its book <u>Sharp Eyes</u> and for reuniting me with a dear friend from the past with whom I had shared a number of botanical adventures. Over time we had lost contact, but once we re-found each other **Frank Knight** agreed to write the foreword for this book

And last but not least I want to recognize the support for the project from family and friends in many ways. My wife **Sandy, all of my six children, Mr. And Mrs. Paul Horwitiz, Mr. and Mrs. Dan Pappone, Mr. James Baird, Mr. Frank Knight, and Mr. and Mrs. David Leslie, Mrs. Jeptha Wade, Martha Hoar, Mr. and Mrs. Hugh Masterman and the Littleton Conservation Trust** Without their steadfast support this book would not have seen the light of day. A special thanks to **George Marrash** for his computer savvy and assistance.

PREFACE

The purpose of this book is to open people's eyes to the world in which plants live. People tend to forget or perhaps don't even know that plants, like people, struggle daily to get enough materials from the environment to survive and perhaps prosper. Somehow plants seem to be alien beings to us rather than respected neighbors and friends.

Botany, as generally presented in school, is generally focused on taxonomy and the useful things we can get from plants rather than on the lifeways of these beings. Although trained as a zoologist and educator, I have come to truly appreciate plants as fellow beings on this planet This is due in large part to the fascination my first born had with plants from his earliest toddler days. In mornings he would go out into the garden and come back with detailed observations on how much different plants had grown overnight, how big the squash fruits were getting, the changing color of the ripening tomatoes and the like. A bit older, he would carry a potted plant around like other young-sters carry a teddy bear. As a teenager he all but completely memorized Bailey's Cyclopedia of Horticulture and he became an expert on seed identifi-cation winning a national 4H competition on the subject. He then went on an orchid collecting trip to Guatemala with Tufts University students. In college he majored in botany and continued his life long fascination with plants until his untimely death at twenty eight. I absorbed much plant lore from him.

I also had some marvelous formal and informal botany teachers during my own education. Dr. Wendell Camp, worldwide plant explorer and a teacher at the University of Connecticut laid basic groundwork. Leonard Bradley, self—taught field botanist extraordinaire with the National Audubon Society and a gifted teacher provided much field information. May Theilgaard Watt's writings and lectures on plant biology and reading the landscape further rounded out my own learning and interests.

To all these people I am deeply indebted and I truly hope this modest book will help carry forth the enthusiasm for the plant world that each of them showed.

In the book you will find three major sections. The first five chapters present a general understanding of the lives of plants.

Chapters 6,7,and 8 focus on ways to record observations and templates and blank pages to help you get started recording different kind of things about plant lives. Chapter 8 is a beginning life history outline to guide your observations and perhaps help you create observation templates of your own.

The Appendices are fairly extensive and help you with knowledge, skills, and tools you may want in your observing and there is also a section of further reading for those who want to delve more deeply into information that others have gathered.

It is my fervent hope that the reader will indeed find joy in plant observing and discover a new avocation that will occupy you for many years to come.

Charles E. Roth
2005
Fitzwilliam, NH

I

GENERAL UNDERSTANDING OF PLANTS

"So far as seeing things is an art, it is the art of keeping your eyes and ears open. The art of nature is all in the direction of concealment...Power of attention and a mind sensitive to outward objects, in these lies the secret of seeing things. Can you bring all your faculties to the front, like a house with many faces at the doors and windows; or do you live retired within yourself, shut up in your own meditations? The thinker puts all the powers of his mind in reflection: the observer puts all the powers of his mind in perception; every faculty is directed outward; the whole mind sees through the eye and hears through the ear. He has an objective turn of mind as opposed to a subjective. A person with the latter turn of mind sees little. If you are occupied with your own thoughts, you may go through a museum of curiosities and observe nothing.

John Burroughs, from *The Art of Seeing Things*

1

THE JOY OF
PLANT WATCHING

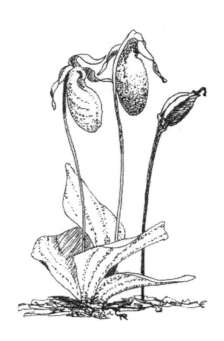

From the dimmest emergence of the conscious human mind in prehistoric times, there has been an awareness of plants. Members of the simplest of human cultures have probed the plant life about them and discovered food, medicine, fiber tool, and also sometimes incurred irritation or even death from plant poisons. As civilizations emerged, they did so borne by an agricultural revolution made possible by subtle observation and manipulation of wild plants over long periods of time. These growing civilizations added new insights to the lore of plant manipulation.

Plants are perceived by people quite differently than are animals. More similar to people, animals are often looked upon as somehow more alive, more deserving of human caring, whereas plants are considered as things, alive yes, but less animate, to be used as basic resources or to provide aesthetic pleasures in the home or as landscape features. Today, many people are interested in plants for gardens and home decorations, but far fewer are acquainted with the daily lives of our wild plant neighbors. Many who do have a nodding acquaintance with wildings generally know only those with conspicuous flowers or the common trees. At that, their knowledge is generally confined to the name and general habitat where the plant may be found.

There is much, much more to be known about the plants around us. Their lives are as complex as those of animals, although their life-ways are different and their activities often proceed at a far slower pace. It is not surprising that in our culture, with its penchant for a stepped-up pace of life, plants are perceived as rather static and boring. On the other hand, many people seek to slow down their own pace, at least occasionally, and getting to know plant life on a more intimate and detailed basis provides one way to get into a more relaxed frame of mind. Indeed, learning to know more about our plant neighbors can become a great source of joy

Plants are borne, grow, mature, grow old, and die. They compete with one another for living space and other basic resource. They have developed diverse strategies for reproducing their kin and expanding their numbers into new sites. In many cases they have co-evolved with animal species to achieve survival. Beautiful as our plant neighbors re, their many adaptation to life on this planet provide an additional source of delight for those of us who gain the skills needed for exploring their lives. Using such skills, we can discover that plants are not mere objects but real living beings.

Many people are aware that a number of animal species are threatened with extinction. Fewer realize that even more plant species are similarly threatened, with many extinctions already, as the human race, increasing in numbers, alters landscapes to meet perceived needs or desires, thus destroying plant habitats. We have only the sparsest knowledge of the specific need for growth and reproduction of most of the threatened species. Lacking such knowledge, the chances of preserving any such species as viable wild populations become highly limited. Amateur plant watcher, discovering ever more about the life histories and habitat requirements of a wide range of species, increase the chances of more species surviving well into the future. Such survival is desirable because of plants' inherent right to pursue their evolution and survival here on Earth and their potential to contribute to human comfort and survival.

This book focuses on how you can discover facts about plants living untended in the wild. You will be helped to become familiar both with individuals and sample populations of species so you can gain a fuller picture of the basic life cycles and survival strategies of those plants. You will also be encouraged to explore the specifics of the habitat in which a species thrives, seek out the factors that seem critical to both survival and good living; and learn about other species it regularly associates with, and how accidental or obligatory such associations are.

One of the advantages of studying plants, as opposed to pursuing most animals, is that they don't run away from you. Unless it has been consumed or died, you can return again and again to the same site and fin the plant you have been watching. Therefore, you can ramble about you community making plant acquaintances and then return over and over to visit them, thus deepening you friendship and enriching your knowledge and understanding of them.

From the first time you begin to look up the name of a plant that has intrigued you, you will encounter the language of the botanist. As with any specialized field, botany has developed its own specialized terms that tend to bewilder and even put off the uninitiated. The value of that special terminology is that it has specificity of meaning. Unfortunately, because of being rooted in the ancient languages of Latin and classical Greek, this special vocabulary tends to leave the average person today more than a little frustrated. The more involved you get in observing plants, the more you will also want to read the works of others, thus raising your level of enjoyment as you acquire the vocabulary of botany. This book makes a bridge between everyday English and botanese. Botanical definitions are offered in the context of the sentence and will usually be followed by the botanical terms in *italics* and/or parentheses. Thereafter the botanical term may be used.

There is much to be said for observing plants for sheer aesthetic enjoyment—their colors, forms, patterns, and scents. It is fervently hoped that in becoming more deeply involved with plants you will never lose your capacity for such enjoyment by having it blunted by an overly zealous commitment to "scientific objectivity."

On the other hand, aesthetic appreciation of plants can be enriched through a deeper intellectual understanding of plants' lifeways. Throughout this book, we are interested in plant watching, which means learning to "see" the plant throughout its life cycle and developing perceptual skills that man an individual species stand out from the more or less uniformly colored and heavily patterned background. Equipped with such skill, you will experience continuous amazement.

PLANT SPOTTING TECHNIQUES

In one sense, spotting plants is easy since they are all around us, even in the heart of most cities. We quickly detect many flowers because their form and color create sharp contrasts with the rest of the plant and the general background. Indeed, survival of many plant species depends upon their flowers being readily seen by those species of animals that are essential to pollination.

For plants without conspicuous flowers, or even for flowering species outside their flowering season, the situation is quite different. The plants tend to become submerged into a more or less common ground of green, yellow, or brown, depending on their location or the season. Spotting a particular species in such settings takes practice and experience.

Science seems to indicate that we have an almost limitless capacity for storing all the visual images to which we are exposed and for recognizing most of them if we see them again. However, in order to be able to call up their appearance to our conscious mind for verbal communication we have to have given conscious word labels to those visual images. To communicate them to others we must have associated those images with appropriate language, because visual and language memories normally operate in different hemispheres of our brain.

What does this have to do with ability to observe plants in the field? We all tend to see according to what we know or believe. It's not just light, color, shape texture, line, patters, similarities, contrasts, and movement that form the language of vision and that registers on our retina; it is what our brain makes of this information and how it is stored in terms of our own personal language. Theoretical physicist Albert Einstein is reputed to have said that you cannot make an observation unless you have a theory to bring to bear on what you are looking at. What our mind tends to focus on from among the multiplicity of visual stimuli that arrives there is guided by our accumulated experiences, stored information, private interest, and entrenched beliefs. This all boils down to the need to prepare yourself to see certain plants before you go afield.

The idea is to prepare yourself so that particular plants can get your attention. Philosopher William James wrote: "Everyone knows what attention is. It is the taking possession by the mind, in clear and vivid form, of one out of what seem several simultaneously possible objects or trains of thought. Focalization, concentration of consciousness, is of the essence. It implies withdrawal from some things in order to deal effectively with others."

A few years ago a friend of mine was working with an inner city community group. One of its projects was to plant flowers at various sites. The participants had poor knowledge of gardening and consequently little of what they planted survived. There was inadequate understanding that the plants had to be tended: essentially they were planted and abandoned. But in front of the community center one hardy plant endured and offered up a cluster of bright flowers. On a return visit to the community center, my friend immediately spotted the flowers and commented on them when she went inside. To her surprise, no one else had "seen" the blooms. They had to be taken outside and shown. They didn't expect the plants to survive and grow. for them. There was no expectation of a flower there. It was not part of their consciousness; therefore, it did not get their attention; to them it simply had not existed.

Similarly, many people take drives in the country and perceive the countryside and the tree-lined road only as a tunnel of green flanked by green mats speckled with colored dots. I suspect that I was once much the same, but today it takes a strong effort for me to register just a tunnel of green, for I see oaks, ashes, maples, and much, much more. The colored dots in the fields are dandelions, mustards, and asters. Each has it distinctive shapes, patterns, and tones, and I have learned to discriminate among them instantaneously. I have never lost my appreciation of the abstract colors and patterns they present, but that appreciation is enriched by a deeper understanding of the plants that create them.

To become aware of the plant species' presence around you, it pays to become familiar with their distinctive patterns and shapes, and often t heir particular hues. Several years ago, on moving into a new house, I noticed a rather coarse "weed" growing in the fencerow. It was a plant I had never "seen" before. Tall, with hollow, jointed stems and large, heart-shaped leaves, it had a thin, papery covering at each joint along the stem. A few minutes with an identification manual revealed that it was a species known as Japanese knotweed or giant polygonum. I was excited to have found this interesting new plant on my property. Even though the guidebook said it was common, I concluded that it must be rare in the area, for surely I would have spotted it before. Much to my chagrin, in succeeding weeks as I visited many old and new haunts I found the species everywhere. It was common! But for me it had never before emerged from the background into my perception.

Some Tricks For Learning To Spot Plants of Interest

Emanating from such experiences and the studies of visual recall is strategy for making certain that species pop out of the background. Spend time carefully studying botanical illustrations—either good drawings or photographs—and memorizing the distinctive patterns, shapes, and colors of a plant. Also, from the text, become familiar with the habitat preferences of a species so that you will know where to begin looking for it. Prepared with this information, you may be surprised at how readily you are able to spot the real plants in the field. As you become more familiar with the species, its characteristic hues and changes through the season, spotting individuals or cluster of the species will become even easier. After all, seeing is a transaction between the object and the viewer.

The foregoing strategy reverses the usual use of identification guides whereby you find a plant and then try to determine its identity from the keys and pictures. This strategy presupposes that you are searching for a certain species. A major weakness is that good pictorial reference for many species are not readily available. Some people can create a visual image of the plant from technical botanical word descriptions, but few of us acquire that skill. It is akin to the skill some have of actually hearing music in their minds when reading the notes of a musical score, a product of years of close familiarity with the discipline.

Another approach to spotting plants, equally dependent upon mental set and background information, involves developing strong familiarity with specific sites or habitats. Become thoroughly acquainted with the shapes, patterns, and hues of the predominant plants that grow in these places. Then scan the sites for items that contrast with the normal familiar background. As your eyes move around the area, you mind will tend to edit out the familiar to the unfamiliar. You can then focus on a detail that may well reveal itself as a species of interest

With practice, you can sharpen this trainable skill both by fieldwork and by the following indoor activity than be either exercise or game. Make a collection of cut paper shapes or a large collection coins or buttons. Spread most of them out on a table and familiarize you self with the patterns they form. Then, while you are turned away from the table, have a partner slip an odd shape somewhere onto the table. Then have the partner give a signal and time how long it takes after you turn around to spot the new object. As a game you and your partner can reverse roles. Compete with yourself or your companion to reduce the time needed to spot the new object. You can build the skill and challenge by making the added items more and more similar to the other shapes and colors on the table.

When you take your improved skill into the field, expect to progress the same way you did in the game—that is, from the most obvious differences to those much more subtle. You will find that your developing skill will be useful not only in spotting new species but also in noting changes within familiar species. You will spot seasonal changes, and you may even learn to spot genetic variants among common species.

Certain groups of plants—grasses, goldenrods, aster, mosses, and a number of others—are often bypassed by people as being too difficult to explore. This is unfortunate, since these groups include many interesting species. In each of these groups there are a number of distinctive species that are quite easy to distinguish from the rest. Become familiar with at least these more readily identifiable ones and don't be disturbed that you don't yet distinguish all their relatives.

As you become more familiar with some of the once-difficult-to-separate species will become more distinguishable. Your growing skill in subtle discrimination of characteristic will make recognition easier. Proceed gradually and before long you will find that the group is much less confusing than you were once led to believe. To be sure, there will be some real puzzlers, but chances are they are confusing to the professional experts as well Often as not, that is because the genetic status of the species is not clear.

As with all skill development, learning to spot plant species in the field takes practice and persistence. Almost always there is a period of frustration, a time when I seems as though you will never learn. Then all at once there comes a breakthrough and things begin to come into focus. This is the so called "learning curve." After a little more honing of the skill, you begin to wonder how you ever could have been so blind. Elation comes as you realize how much more there is to this beautiful planet than you had ever previously imagined. This may even be followed by a certain missionary zeal as you try to help others make a similar discovery for themselves. Clearly there is a touch of that behind the writing of this book!

Once you start watching plants, what are you really watching for? For enjoyment, of course, but also to learn more out of curiosity about the life of a fellow traveler on this solar-orbiting space station. Since our focus for the book is not the laboratory with its electron microscopes and other gadgetry for probing the inner workings of plants, our attention here is on the whole integrated plant organism and its relationships to the physical and biological environment in which it grows.

WHAT THIS BOOK HELPS YOU DO

This book will encourage you to gather life history information, which is only partially known for most species. The tendency among scientists and lay people alike has been to examine thoroughly a few species in each plant group while gathering only spotty information about their kin. As part of life history investigations, this book can help you explore natural phenomena that recur periodically as season change—for example, blossoming, fruiting, and leaf unfurling. *Phenology* is the science of seasonal changes in plants and animals,

Another major area of exploration is searching for environmental tolerances, requirements and responses of plants or plant species. This branch of ecology, *autecology*. focuses on an individual organisms or species as its major unit of concern. This book includes material on how to go about determining other plant species with which a given species is likely to be regularly associated. Indeed, sometime you will want to study plant communities themselves as a unit. *Synecology* is the branch of ecology devoted to such synthesis of organisms sharing habitats.

Investigations of all these aspects of a plant's lifeway are inter-related and of equal importance even though they have not been equally well studied. When taking a broad look at the many plants of an area, we speak of them as vegetation. Pressures of time and the large size of many units of vegetation have led to techniques for studying vegetation directly without concern for4 the nature of the species that compose it. Such studies are based on the size and shape of the plants, whether they are evergreen or deciduous, softly herbaceous or had and woody, and on other characteristics comprising life forms. Description of vegetation is a convenient shorthand way of making rather superficial analysis to deduce the botanical character of a region, but it leaves a great deal of exploration for the amateur or professional field botanist. Many conclusions based on plant communities a study units are suspect because of the limited information that exists about the ecological need of component species. Plant ecologist Henry Oosting noted in his now classic work, *The Study of Plant Communities:* "Just as the study of vegetation must remain more or less superficial without a solid knowledge of the flora, so will interpretation and explanations be limited by the amount of autecological information available about the species and their environments. Physiological-ecological investigations in the field and under natural condition constantly modify synecological conclusions that have been made deductively, or they suggest new interpretations and investigations." The amateur field botanist can make contributions to just such studies and from them derive a hobby filled with joy and satisfaction.

This book will also provide you with some recording/journaling activities that will help you keep track of your many observations and focus your perceptions.

2

ASSEMBLING
LIFE HISTORIES

Beautiful flowers or striking foliage usually call attention to a particular plant, but seldom do we have an accurate perception of the whole plant at any given time in its life. Although plants are all around us, in many ways they remain little green alien creatures. Since the don't move about like most animals, communicate in the way animals do, or normally respond quickly to environmental stimuli, people tend to think of them as almost inanimate objects.

However, plants are living things. They develop from tiny embryos into fragile young, mature over time, reproduce, and eventually die. The overall pattern of their life histories is much the same as an animal's although the details differ significantly.

To become intimately familiar with plants, either as species or as distinctive components of local vegetation, you must understand at least the broad outline of each species' life history. The pattern of their lives determines what they are going affect and how they will be affected by other species.

Although plants may superficially appear quite simple, their life ways are often remarkably complex. Over the millennia they have often co-evolved intricate relationships with animal species as well as with other plants. Some species have been studied extensively and their life histories are well detailed, but for the majority of species life history information is quite fragmentary. Certain stages have been carefully chronicled while other remain virtually unstudied.

Assembling information necessary to creating a full portrait of a species is something journal keepers and we amateur field botanists can devote ourselves to throughout a lifetime. There will always be something new to discover and many opportunities to see at firsthand aspects of a species' activities. It is extremely doubtful that a complete life history has yet been written about any species; indeed, it is unlikely that one can ever be written. Condition change readily and plants respond to them, often causing localized alterations in the basic life history pattern of a species.

The challenge of life is seldom easy for any species. Even though most plants manufacture their own food (we say they are *autotrophic,* literally "self-feeding"). They still must get the basic raw materials from the surrounding environment. They must get enough water and minerals to replace what is lost in the day to day living process, and they must avoid excessive heat from the sun. They have to face competition from the leaves, stems, and roots of other species and must cope with the appetites of a broad spectrum of animal species. Local weather may alter the environment of the species for better or worse. Over time, plants have met these and other challenges in quite distinctive ways.

MAJOR PATTERNS OF LIFEWAYS

There are many ways in which one might classify the life patterns of plants. For the purpose of thing in terms of plant life histories, we will focus here on three major patterns of longevity for plants known as annuals, biennials, and perennials. These patterns involve the average time it takes the plant to go through a cycle from germination to reproduction and senescence.

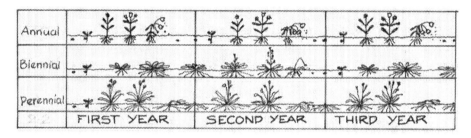

Figure 2-1

Annuals usually complete their life cycle in one growing season, surviving to the next growing season only as dormant seed. This pattern of activity is very successful in colonizing frequently disturbed soils. Annuals generally have relatively rapid growth rates and regenerate almost entirely by seed.

Biennials usually complete their life cycle in two growing seasons. Their first year is devoted to *vegetative growth* (roots, stems, and leaves) usually producing a rosette of leaves that grows close to the ground. *Photosynthates*, products of photosynthesis, are stored in the root system over the winter. During the following growing season most of the growth is concentrated on reproductive structures—namely flowers. fruits. seeds. and their supporting stems After that, the plant will die. Biennials tend to do best in disturbed areas and are often found associated with annuals. Biennials, however, can survive bad times more effectively than annuals and may occasionally extend the vegetative stage for another year or so until they have stored up enough photosynthates to invest in a reproductive season. Once they reproduce, their life is over.

Perennials have an indefinite life span that can extend from three years to centuries. They may take several years to reach sexual maturity and then produces seeds or spores regularly or intermittently for the rest of their lives. Because of their persistence, many perennials have the opportunity to become well established on a site and eventually to become dominant species in the local vegetation. This may take years and many setbacks, but their ability to store photosynthates in good years and draw upon them in bad ones increases their likelihood of surviving adverse conditions and exploiting favorable ones.

Each of the various patterns of life history conveys advantages and drawbacks for surviving under a given set of conditions. As the field botanist becomes interested in the various strategies for survival in different habitats, the need to become intimately acquainted with the specific life styles of the various species that make up the vegetation in any given habitat becomes increasingly important. It is amazing how little is known about the details of the lives of most of our plants, even the most common ones. The amateur has a broad opportunity to add to the general knowledge of almost any species. It is fun getting to know local species in detail and using your nature journal notes to assemble over time an increasingly detailed revelation of their lives.

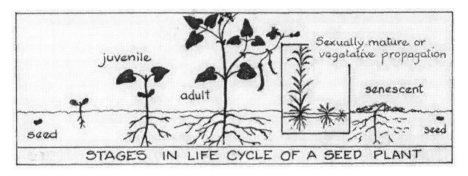

Figure 2-2

Aspects of a Portrait

In the following sections we will examine various aspects of the life history of typical plants and look at questions to be explored uniformly to all groups of plants, for there is too much diversity among these creatures. In the second section of this book you will find a working outline for a plant life history. This will help you organize your observations over the years. Also you will find additional discussion of life history fine points of specific plant groups in the following chapter.

SEEDS AND SPORES

Seed and spores are a good beginning point in the exploration of plant life histories. For most plants they are the primary devices for spanning the generations, surviving difficult times in the environment, reaching new sites to increase populations and providing some mixing of genetic material that may pre-adapt a species to subtle environmental changes. However, plants also have a variety of ways of propagating vegetativly.

Spores are limited to the non-flowering plants; seeds to the flowering ones. Spores differ from seeds in that they lack a pre-formed embryo. Most spores are minute, and the sporophyte plants produce them in prodigious numbers. Study of spores by amateurs is very difficult, requiring access to a microscope and often us of laboratory culturing techniques to get them to germinate under observable conditions.

There are some things regarding spores to be noted by the plant observer. These focus around the structures where the spores are generated and the ways in which the spores are dispersed. By far, the most common method of dispersal is by wind, but there are some species on non-flowering plants that depend upon rain splash to scatter the spores, for example, many mosses. Others have a propulsion mechanism to shoot out the spores. On discovering the history of a particular species, carefully note the method of spore dispersal; it may reveal how individuals of the species get a start in life.

All spores are quite small by our standard but everything is relative. The larger the spores, the less distance they are likely to travel and the shorter the period of time they are likely to remain airborne. It is also worth noting that larger spores have more food reserves than smaller ones and thus more energy for getting a plant established at a new site.

Among the liverworts, spores seldom take long trips but tend to settle relatively close to the parent plants. Some of their near cousins the mosses, have more complex means of spore dispersal that may result in strong ejection of the spores into the atmosphere where air currents may distribute them over considerable distance.

Horsetail *(Equisetum)* spores are interesting in that they have long coiled flaps called *elaters*. These make up the special part of the spore wall. When the spore dries out, the elaters uncoil to create 'sails' that help the spores ride the wind. When spores land in a moist place, their elaters coil up again and the spores germinate.

Most fern spores, which are wind-disseminated, tend to be born in clusters of sporangia called *sori*. Sometimes the sori appear on the undersides of ordinary leaves *(fronds)*, while in other species they are located on special stalks or modified fronds. The arrangement of sori on the fronds often helps in the identification of fern species.

Among most spore bearing plants there is only one type of spore and such species are referred to as being *homosporous*. But among *heterosporous* groups, such as the selaginella and some ferns, there are to different sized spores. The larger ones develop into female plants; the smaller into males.

SEEDS

For most people, seeds are much more familiar than the spores of non-flowering plants and, by and large, they are much easier to explore than spores because of the greater size. Seeds differ from spores in that they contain preformed, embryonic plants. In addition they generally contain significant amounts of stored food that give the embryo a boost in initial growth.

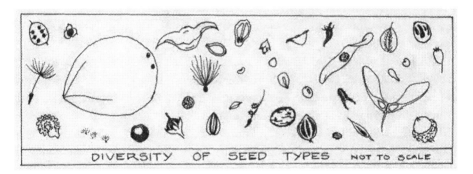

Figure2-3

Seeds very in size from the dust-like seeds of many orchids to the somewhat larger than softball sized coconuts. There is diversity of form as well; much of which is adapted to methods of see dispersal. There are seed with floats, wings, parachutes, and grappling hooks. Sore are wrapped in edible packages (fruits) that will either be eaten by animals with the seeds passing unharmed through the alimentary tract to be deposited in the accompanying, bed of fertilizer, or whose attractive coating itself decays to form fertilizer.

There is much to be learned about the seed of any given species. Seeds are major devices for permitting a plant species to reproduce its kind and thus expand its occupation of appropriate habitat. Thus, seeds deserve some close attention. As plant communities undergo change, the capacity of a species' seed to locate a suitable germination site and get its embryo established and growing may be the deciding factor in determining its place in the type of vegetation that will develop next.

FIELD OBSERVATIONS REGARDING SEEDS

Watch and time the following items in the field. Mark individual plants with little tags to which you can reference your journal notes.

What is the average time from fertilization of flowering to ripening and dispersal of a plant's seeds. If you can, match this information with data on temperature and rainfall. In some cases you may determine that the average ripening time varies from year to year, depending on environmental conditions. In other species the ripening time may be quite constant from year to year, because it is determined by internal biological rhythms. With such plants, seed size may very due to environmental conditions during the internally fixed development time.

What devices does a seed have for its dispersal? Make photos or drawings of the seed and its special adaptations for dispersal. Every species has its own special forms, but there are some common themes. For example, maple trees all have the winged *(samara)* form of dispersal, but each species has wings of different length, width, and angle. Thus, each has different aerodynamic qualities that cause it to disperse slightly differently. You can have fun watching the seeds of different maple species dispersing and noting the varying abilities to get away from the shade of the parent tree.

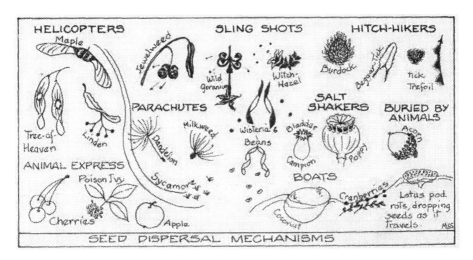

Figure 2-4

There are also many variations on the hook theme, which permits certain seed to catch on animal fur or human clothing and travel to a new area where the animal cleans the seed from its fur. One inventor spent years studying the burdock seed and its crochet-hook barbs. From his studies came the invention of hook-and-loop type closures.

Where do seeds from various species end up? One reason for building a good seed collection of species in your area <see side bar> so you can undertake "scavenger hunts" to see what seeds have made their way to various soil samples. One way is to study the soil sample carefully with a good hand lens and collect as many seeds as possible. Sometimes it helps to put the samples through a series of increasing finer mesh and hunting through each screening for seeds. It's a bit like being an archaeologist sifting a site for human artifacts. A labeled seed collection is a reference for identifying your finds.

A second approach involves putting samples of the soil in trays or flats and germinating the seeds. The task then is to identify the various seedlings. A discussion of germination methods can be found in the section on seedlings.

Some seeds germinate almost as soon as they land on suitable soil. This should be noted whenever you observe it. Many species, however must to through a period of dormancy before they can germinate. This dormancy may be only for a brief cold period or may last for decades, even centuries in some species. A variety of things may break the dormancy—the seed coat may become nicked so that water can penetrate; light may finally get to the seed after long periods in the dark; or soil may warm after a prolonged freezing. Each of these things has an influence on the way seed establish their species in a new location. In many habitats, the soil will be found to hold a fair variety of dormant seeds in what amounts to a seed bank. The bank awaits changes in the environment that will stimulate some of its member species to germinate. The length of the wait and the nature of the changes will determine which component of the seed bank will get their "day in the sun" and thus determine what kind of plant community will next occupy that site.

What enemies does the seed have? For seeds, chance is their best friend and greatest enemy. A plant must produce vast number of seeds just to allow a very few to find suitable germinating conditions. Even fewer of these seeds will survive long enough to mature and reproduce themselves. In addition to the odds of finding proper conditions, the seeds must face a host of other organisms that want to tap the materials and energy stored in the embryo and its nourishing container. Examine seed for evidence of insects that may have bored inside to feed or lay eggs. If you find insects or other invertebrates feed on you seeds, you can send samples of them to scientists at the state university or the county extension service for identification. Be sure to include drawings or photos of these predators in your journal. Note also the birds that feed on those seeds and the small and large mammals. Even where the number of seeds per plant is quire large, these enemies can put such a dent in the number of seeds available to germinate that almost no seedlings may get started in a given year.

What is the average seed production per plant in a given location and year? Like animals, plants have good years and bad. Tag enough specimens of your study species for a representative sample and count the seed production. For species that produce relatively few seeds per plant, such a count is much more feasible than for those that produce thousands of tiny seeds. Nonetheless, the number of seeds in a given year helps establish a clue to that species' reproductive potential and its chances of gaining or retreating as a member of the plant community.

DEVELOP A SEED COLLECTION

A good beginning activity for field botanist is to collect samples of a many different ripe seeds as possible and store each sample in a labeled envelope or plastic baggy. If you can't yet identify the parent plant assign a letter or number to each sample. Each label should contain the location where the seeds were found, the date of collection, and either the name or assigned letter or number. When the seed are well dried so they will not become mold, they can be kept in neatly labeled glass or plastic vials arranged in trays or plastic boxes. If a particular plant of a gene species seems unusual in flower, color, form, or other characteristic, be sure to keep its seeds separate; you may want to try to grow some of them later.

The seed collection will be useful for a variety of things. First of all by studying the seeds you will be able to recognize the species even when you find it some distance from any parent plant. Or you can compare an unknown seed with you labeled collection to help identify it. Second, you can set up experiments with the seeds to determine how long it takes a given species to germinate and also to learn if there are any special conditions that must be met if a given species is to germinate.

You can also try germinating some of the seeds from a given batch over a period of successive years to determine roughly how many years seed of that species remain viable. For some species it is only a year or two; for a few species, like lotus plants, it can be over a thousand years. The germination characteristics and viability of seeds over time are of considerable importance to a species' strategy for survival.

THE SEEDLING OR JUVENILE STAGE

Perhaps the most neglected stage in any plant species life is the juvenile stage, the time between germination and first flowering or sporulation. It is a difficult time in a plant's life, and mortality is generally quire high.

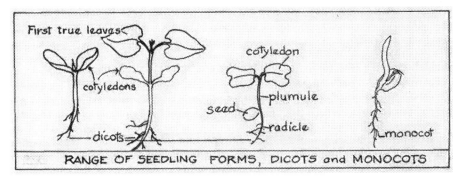

Figure 2-5

There are many things to observe about the early development of a plant. How does the embryonic plant emerge from the seed? Does the root emerge first or do the seed leaves? Is there a considerable time lag between appearance of toot and seed leaves or do they emerge at about the same time? Such details are generally only visible by sprouting seeds between blotters and glass.

As seedlings emerge from the ground photograph or sketch them carefully over a period of several weeks. Be sure to note data about when you begin to see particular seedlings. They will often be quite different in appearance from more mature plants and will frequently have distinctive seed leave, or *cotyledons*. A number will have first leave quire different in form and/or color from more mature ones. Almost no books exist that provide identification keys to seedlings. There are a few booklets on weed species that you will find in the further reading section It is assumed that people either overlook seedlings entirely or can wait until they are mature to identify them.

At first that is what you may have to do. Carefully record the seedlings that interest you and follow their development to mature plants that you can more readily identify. Then in the next growing season you will have the ability to recognize those seedlings by species while they are still small. Being able to recognize seedlings helps determine which plant species are trying to establish themselves in an area. It is not unusual for all the seedlings of a particular species to die in an area year after year until some change in the surroundings creates altered condition that will permit some of the seedlings to become well established and survive. By following the successes of a selected species' seedlings in various habitats and years, you may learn something of the conditions needed for them to succeed.

In order for seedlings to survive, they generally have to maximize their surface area successfully both above and below ground. This is necessary if they are to tap the most basic resources possible. Shallow-rooted seedling will spread a network of rootlets but are very vulnerable to drought or competition from the roots of better—established plants. Tap-rooted species will send their roots downward to perhaps more secure sources of moisture and minerals. These seedlings may survive several seasons of having their aerial parts damaged or removed completely. As long as their growth center—just below ground—remains intact, they may appear to have been destroyed only to reappear again later in the season or in the next year. Some seedlings, particularly or tree species, are remarkably persistent over a period of years before they get a chance to make significant growth.

Seedlings are especially vulnerable to predation by a host of organisms. As many as possible of these should be recorded for any species under study. The outer surface of a tender stem has very little deposits of corky material to protect from the invasion of fungi (the dreaded "damping off" disease of gardeners' seedlings); mechanical injury from passing of animals; the falling of limbs, and the like. Depending upon the species, however, the biggest threats to survival are usually too much or too little light or too much or too little water. The needs of seedling may be quite different than the needs of mature plants, and these should be determined. Condition for successful seedling establishment and growth may be much more critical to a species than its apparent adult preference. Indeed, the environment of an adult plant may be somewhat misleading and terns of that species' needs. As adults, individual species may be able to tolerate a wide range of condition while as seedlings their environmental tolerance may be much more limited and critical.

In the field, it is difficult to assess accurately a seedling's specific environmental needs. That must usually be done in the greenhouse or laboratory under carefully controlled condition with many batches of seedlings. However, field studies of light, pH, moisture, and mineral nutrients around the seedlings will point to parameter to be later confirmed or denied by the controlled studies.

There are a number of other ecologically important matters to be noted by following a seedling's development in the field. *On average, how long after germination do the first true leaves appear? How much growth of stem occurs between each new leaf: If the species is herbaceous, are there a particular number of leaves that must develop before the plant matures and produces flowers? Are young leaves significantly different in shape and size from older ones? How old is the seedling before it develops a more fibrous or corky stem covering to add to its protection? Does this coincide with a time when mortality among the seedlings seems to be reduced?*

REPRODUCTIVE MATURITY

After an appropriate period of development, each species of plant may reproduce if is in a proper habitat and fortune smiles. Some species will grow and survive outside their preferred home but never reproduce there although they seem appropriately mature. Annual and biennial species generally go through their growth and development phase, and then flower and shortly thereafter die. However, perennials are more complex in their reproductive patterns. Many utilize both vegetative modes such as runners, stolons, bulbs, and the

like, and sexual modes—such as flowers, fruits, and seeds. They may reproduce for several years or more entirely by vegetative means, and then proceed
to flower. They may reproduce regularly by both means. A bad season's stress
may trigger greatest flowering. Apparently such species respond to stress by
using sexual mode, which creates offspring of wider genetic variation than
vegetative reproduction and provides opportunities for dispersal beyond the
area of stress. The astute plant watcher keeps good track of what is happening
reproductively with each of the species that hold his or her attention and real-
izes that what happens in any given year is not necessarily typical of those species.

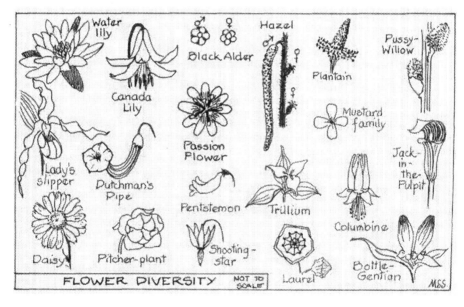

Figure 2-6

The World of Flowers

For most species, the flowers are their best-known features. The more colorful
or bizarre the form, the greater the likelihood that they have been carefully
studied—yet new things are being discovered about flowers all the time. For
instance, it has relatively recently been discovered that a number of plants that
live in arctic climates or flower in the cool of early spring act as miniature solar
reflectors that focus the sun's warmth over the center of the flower. Studies

with delicate temperature sensors show these spots to be several degrees warmer than the surrounding air. This proves very attractive to local flying insects. The plants profit because the insects that take advantage of the warmth get covered with pollen and thus transfer it from plant to plant. It is a nice example of the phenomenon or co-evolution, whereby two very different life forms slowly evolve together for mutual benefit.

It has also been discovered that flowers may appear quite differently to certain insects than they do to us. We do not perceive light energy in the ultraviolet range, but many insects, particularly bees, do. Photographs taken with ultraviolet-sensitive film have revealed that some flowers that seem uniformly colored to us actually have definite patterns that can be seen by those organisms sensitive to ultraviolet. These patterns often direct an insect's attention to those part of the flower that will most benefit the insect in its search for food and thus create the highest chance of the plant being pollinated—another indication of co-evolution at work.

There are many aspects of flowering for the plant observer to note. *Does the flower remain open around the clock once it unfolds from the bud, or does it open and close according to regular time pattern?* Some species are so specific in the timing of their opening and closing that it is possible for gardeners to plant floral clocks that have a regular succession of openings and closing throughout the day and to some extent at night. Once you become familiar with the habits of certain species, you can tell roughly what time of day it is those species in bloom do or do not have their flowers open—but don't let cloudy days fool you.

How long does an individual blossom last? Is its longevity essentially a built in period of growth or does its demise start soon after pollination? This isn't always easy to determine; you may have to experiment by mechanically preventing pollination, such as by encasing the blooms in mesh bags.

What adaptations does the plant have for either self—or cross-fertilization? The eggs, or *ovules,* in the ovary of a flower can be fertilized by pollen from the stamens of any flower of the same species, including the ones in the very flower on which they are located. Indeed, many species self-pollinate regularly, while other go to elaborate lengths to assure that pollen from different plants of the same species accomplish the fertilization. This may mean that the pollen grains in a given flower mature at a different rate from its ovules; that some flowers produce only pollen or only ovules; or that male and female flowers may occur on separate plants.

As you find flowers in bloom, carefully note the presence or absence of stamens; and if stamens are present check them and note when pollen grains appear and how long they are present. Pollen grains are often bizarre when seen magnified. Check them with a 10x magnifier, or a microscope, and sketch or photograph the pollen grains. Pollen grains that don't land on a flower's *pistil* may survive intact for hundred of centuries particularly if they land on an acid bog. Scientists have been able to determine the abundance of some species over time by separating pollen from cores of peat extracted from such bogs. The science of determining changing plant communities of the distant past using the pollen record of bogs is call *palynology.*

When does the flower produce odor or nectar if it does? Many flowers generate scents or liquid nectars that attract certain species of insects. In the visits the insects collect pollen deliberately or accidentally pick it up on their bodies and carry it to other flowers, thus enhancing the changes of the plant's pollination. Some produce the odor or, species that depend upon wind pollination generally lack either odor or nectar and produce much more pollen than do insect-pollinated plants.

The odors that some flowers produce do not smell sweet but are more like the foul odors of carrion. Examples include skunk cabbage, carrion flower, and stinkhorn mushrooms. Such species tend to depend more on species of flies for their pollination than on the bees and butterflies we usually associate with that task. There are also many other insect groups that may get involved in pollination. Note the kinds you see visiting the blossoms and identify them if you can. If they are unfamiliar collect one or two voucher specimens and preserve them. They can then be sent to the department of entomology at a state university for identification. Be sure to have good data for each specimen (date, location, plants associated with it, collector's name) The university people will normally, want to keep the specimens. If you have questions about preparing the specimens, refer to a good field guide to insects at you local library, or even better, buy on for continuing use. Watching insects can be on of the great joys of observing plant lifeways.

What is the flowering period? Flowering is affected by a variety of environmental factors, but for most temperate-zone species the main stimulating factors are fairly constant, such as changing length of day or night. In more extreme environments, such as deserts, the process may be triggered by a sudden influx of moisture. For the plant observer it is more to the point to first record a species' flowering sequence over a period of years and then try to determine whether it is primarily attuned to recurring climatic constants or to more changeable local weather conditions. To get good information about flowering times you will want to gather data from several study plots (see Appendix D). Note when the first blossom opens, add data on when half the plants in the study areas are in bloom, and when the last blossom bud opens. If you are really eager, you may also want to add data on when one quarter and three quarters of the blossoms in the study area are open. This data can then be plotted on a calendar to crate a flowering chart for the areas' species in any given year. Such information might look like Figure 2.8. Also see guided journaling project Keeping Bloom Calendars.

Record-keeping of the timing of various events in a plant's life history (like flowering and the linking of such events to factors of weather, climate, and soils are called *phenology*. Ecologist Paul Shepard writes "Phenology, like taxonomy, in contrast to the more trendy forms of nature study in behavior or ecology, does not have a lively press. But it is what the mature naturalist finally comes to. It is not that these topics are actually less dynamic than the more dramatic aspects of nature, gut that their liveliness depends on a deeper understanding and a more refined sense of mystery"

Collecting phenological records is clearly within the realm of the amateur plant observer. There has been a tendency for amateurs to go for "first and last" records, such as the first bluebird of spring and the last rose of summer. But much more valuable is information on when the majority of a species is involved in a given activity. First and last records may set the outer limits of a species' particular activity pattern, but they generally are records of the exceptions rather than the rule. Their major value may be in suggesting the limits of present adaptability to prevailing conditions.

Date	Species	Event
		tips of leaves first appear above ground
		folded leaves completely out of ground
		leaves completely unfurled
		flower buds appear above leaves
		first flower opens
	PHENOLOGICAL RECORD FORM	

Figure 2-7

What is the average number of blossoms per plant? Gathering such informa-tion will require some patience at counting or the recruitment of some friends to help. In many cases you will have to take some standard samples and deal with the number of flowers in the sample. This figure will vary considerably from year to year and location to location. It's important to have good infor-mation on rainfall, temperature, soil conditions, and changing exposure to light or shade to correlate with your blossoming data.

In some cases, you may also want to note the percentage of blossoms that go unfertilized. There may be good bloom, but pollinator populations may b down for a variety of reasons so that few seeds will actually be produced. It is even possible for a year of relatively low number of bloom numbers to end up with a higher set of seed because pollination percentage is high. The plant observer should keep constantly alert for such events. The information helps determine the reproductive efficiency of the plants and this information may be crucial where trying to determine conservation strategies for plants that are becoming threatened or endangered.

What factors injure the flower buds and cause them to self-destruct? Flower buds are often more sensitive to various environmental insults than is the plant as a whole. Frost, drought, dessication from wind, mechanical damage from wind, passing animals, or the onslaught of certain insects—all can prevent flower buds from doing their job. Such injuries should be noted for the species you are studying. *What specific temperatures are deadly? What relative humidity condi-tions are lethal to the bud?* Such things will be most noticeable with species at the edges of their normal range of distribution. The frequency of occurrence of such conditions over a span of years may say a great deal about the likelihood of whether a species will become well established in an area or die out.

What is the sequence of opening of individual blossoms in a cluster? Some clus-ters have all blossoms open at the same time, others open sequentially from the tip down to the base, and still others open just the reverse. A few, like tea-sel, begin opening at the middle of the cluster and work outwards in both directions. For many species you may find that just as there is a definite math-ematical sequencing to the blossom and leaf arrangements on a branch or stalk, so too is there and orderly sequence of blossom opening. Keep track also of how long it takes for a whole cluster to go through the bloom cycle and which blossoms are most likely to be successfully pollinated.

What is the sequence of loss of flower parts as their fertilized flower transforms into the fruit? The transformation from flower to fruit is a fascination one that few people ever observe very closely. Various parts of the flower will be shed in sequence to become parts of the "organic rain" that settles on the ground. Petals, sepals, and stamens tend to be lost, and the expanding ovary with its developing seeds may absorb other flower parts, like the pistil. Familiarize yourself with the various flower parts and then carefully record the fate of each as the transformation occurs

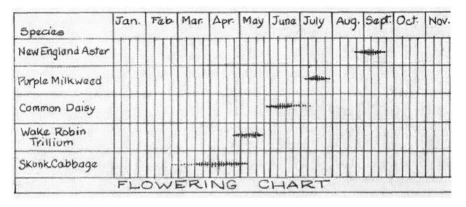

Figure 2-8

FRUITS

It is very difficult to separate flowering from development of fruit since it is a continuous development of some of the flower parts. Botanically. A fruit is the mature ovary of the plant along with its included seeds, and occasionally with neighboring flower parts incorporated (as in strawberries and pineapples). Although conifers bear cones that are not technically fruits, we include consideration of them here for convenience.

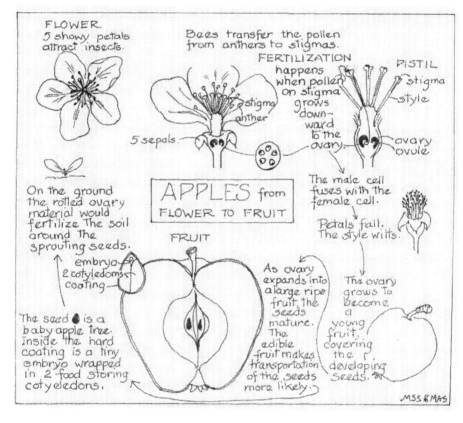

Figure 2-9

How long does it take for the ovary to develop from the flower to mature state for seed dispersal? It is interesting to keep a photographic or sketched record of the development of various fruits. Keep track of any insects or fungi that invade the developing fruits, for they are often responsible for preventing a large percentage of ovaries from developing into mature fruits with viable seeds. It is good to establish a sample of marked ovaries and determine what percent of them reach maturity in any given year. It gives another piece of information for determining reproductive success in any given year.

What is the method of seed release from the fruit? In some species the outer husk of the fruit dries and splits releasing the seeds; in other, there is an increase in water intake that stretches the covering until the slightest touch will force it to burst open and expel the seeds, as with the various species of tough-me-not (Impatiens). Other species depend upon the feeding activities of animals to free the seed. Some species have coverings that decay to create a nutrient-rich bed for the now exposed seed or seeds. Pinecones usually must dry out so that the cone scales extend to release the winged seeds, with a few species requiring the heat of fire to bring about the opening of the cone scales.

What is the average number of seeds per fruit and what is the average number of fruits per plant? The number of seeds per fruit is normally quite constant and genetically determined, but the number of fruits per plant will depend on a number of factors relative to a particular growing season. It is an indication of the plant's reproductive potential in a given year.

VEGETATIVE REPRODUCTION

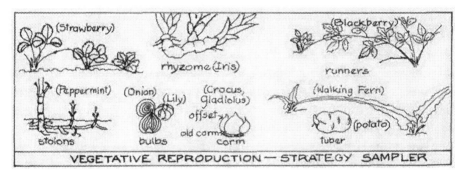

Figure 2-10

Flowers are only one way in which a plant may reproduce itself. Flowers are the sexual mode that provides for a genetic diversity in the offspring; thus allowing for some adaptation to slightly altered environments. Flowers create *disseminules* (fruits and seeds or spores)that help new individuals move some distance from the parent plants. But many species also have various ways of reproducing asexually by vegetative reproduction of roots, stems, or leaves. These offspring have the same genetic makeup as their parents. This is quite satisfactory as long as living conditions remain within the same range that the parent plants need. Such vegetative offspring of the same genetic makeup are often known as *clones*.

In many kinds of vegetative reproduction, the new plant remains attached to the parent for indefinite periods of time, so it; is often difficult to determine whether we are dealing with an individual plant or many. Whole hillsides of aspen trees *(Populus)* may be interconnected clones from one tree that arrived as a seed. You may have seen symmetrical clumps of sumac *(Rhus)* along road-sides that are high in the center and taper to the edges. These too are clones clumps. The tallest individuals in the center are the oldest and the increasingly shorter individuals represent progressively younger individuals. It is highly likely that they are all interconnected below the ground.

In developing a full account of a plant's life history, you should record any types of vegetative reproduction. Most of them are below ground activities, but there are a variety of aboveground structures that should be noted. Straw-berries, for example, send out runners *(stolons)* that eventually tough ground, send down roots, and develop a new stem, leaves, and other appropriate struc-tures; many roses, raspberries, viburnums, and other plants will root if a stem tip bends over and touches the ground. Some ferns produce little bulblets on the leaves that drop off and grow. Species of *Kalanchoe* form little plants along the leaf margins that will drop off and grow and some ferns such as walking ferns (*Camptosorus rhizophyllus*) form new plants when the extended leaf tip touches the ground. Many aquatic plants reproduce vegetatively. The tiny duckweed (*Lemna*) that tend to cover our waterways in summer like green confetti are true flowering plants yet they seldom bloom, reproducing instead almost entirely by budding off from the existing leaves.

Plants with both vegetative and sexual reproduction have increased their options and thus their chances of expanding their populations through a wide range of conditions. Where it is hard for seedlings to get established, vegeta-tive offspring partially subsidized by their connection to the parent for a sub-stantial period of growth allow the plant to expand into new, unexploited territory. Seed are the high-risk adventurers, vegetative offspring the conser-vative stay-at-homes.

SPORE-PRODUCING NONFLOWERING PLANTS

Mosses, liverworts, club mosses, horsetails, and ferns produce fruiting bodies that generate spores. Keep watch on each species in your area and note when these fruiting bodies first appear; how long it takes for mature spores to appear; how the spore are released; and what happens to the used fruiting bodies. Be sure to not ethe weather condition and microclimate where the plants are located in order to be able to correlate plant activity with environmental condition. With many of the ferns, the observer has to b e very alert and systematic as the fruiting bodies (*sori*) for on the undersides of the fronds. Other fern species bear their sori on separate fruiting fronds. Note when these appear and what ultimately happens to them. Some of the non-flowering plants also have vegetative means of reproduction. Leaflets may break off and develop into new plants; this is particularly true of plants subject to trampling by animals. Keep alert for these vegetative plants and record them in your journal.

PATTERNS OF GROWTH

The genetic heritage of a species builds into its development certain basic patterns such as general leaf shape, size, growth habit, fruiting time, and other such structural and behavioral adaptations. Expression of the genetic heritage will often be altered by local environmental factors. Indeed, if the environmental factors are consistent enough, they may favor some genetic alterations that give rise to slight variations in the local population. These variations are not great enough to warrant new species status but are enough to recognize it properly as a local variety *(ecotype)*. Familiarity with a species in one geographical area is no guarantee that the same species will respond or develop in the same way elsewhere, but that is part of the challenge of plant observing.

We can think of most flowering plants as leading dual lives—one above ground, the other below. As a seed first sprouts, a growing point sends a *radicle* downward to start developing the root system; and adjacent growing point sends the *plumule* upward to develop the stem, leaves, and later flowers and fruits. The developing plant attempts constantly to increase contact with the environment in order to take in a larger and larger share of the raw materials it needs for living—namely air, water, and mineral nutrients. These raw materials in turn allow the plant to increase in size and environmental contact up to the limits imposed by its current genetic constitution and any constraints imposed by the environment.

STEMS AND LEAVES

Certain parts of many plants, aside from the fruiting bodies, seem almost to have separate lives of their own. With most animal species we usually think of death as coming to the whole organism at once. With plants this is true of annuals and biennials, but with perennials, it is different. Leaves, and often stems, die annually, but the underground parts, specialized stems, and roots live on indefinitely and send up new sprouts each year

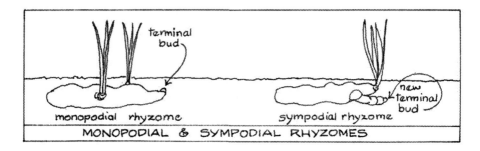

Figure 2-11

Many of these species are very long lived but do eventually seem to loose vigor and die. On the other hand, there are those that live for centuries and appear immortal. It is mind—boggling to realize that in some of the remaining wetlands of a place like Plymouth, Massachusetts there are humble skunk cabbage plats alive today that were probably poking up their mottled hood when the Pilgrims arrived and for many years before.

As a young stem grows upwards, you will be able to note small bumps that are the precursors of leaves. In time their cell will differentiate into the shapes that make up a typical leaf. As leaves form and the stem continues to grow at the tip, new bumps will form at the angle (*axil*) between the leaf and the stem. Those bumps will become *axillary buds* that may develop into branches, flowers, new leaves, or a combination thereof. Because the growing tip is the apex, or top, of the stem, it should not be surprising that buds that form there are called apical, or terminal, buds.

As you observe a developing plant, keep track of the number of leaves and buds that appear on the stem. Eventually the plant will stop growing upward. *Are there a reasonably consistent number of leaves on any given stem at the time it stops its upward growth?* For some species this will be the case, in others not. *Does there appear to be a relationship between number of leaves on a plant and its environmental conditions: or, under unfavorable conditions, does the plant stick to a basic number of leaves but reflect the poor conditions in smaller leaf size and less robust stems?* Does the plant have to have reached a particular development of stems and leaves before it produces flower buds? You may find that the differences you discover show correlation with annual, biennial, or perennial life styles.

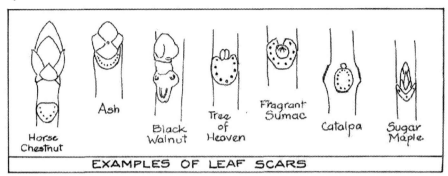

EXAMPLES OF LEAF SCARS

Figure 2-12

In the study area, how long does it take a shoot or sapling of a species to reach average maximum height? This will be much easier to determine in annuals and biennials than in woody perennials such as redwood and sequoias, which may continue upward growth for centuries.

What factors seem most to affect rate of growth and/or premature cessation of growth? If you compare rates of growth of annual plants, you may find that they vary from year to year in ways you can correlate with information on temperature, rainfall, mineral depletion, and other environmental factors. Seen in the context of communities of plants, these growth factors can be very important. For example, sideways growth of tree branches eventually creates a closed forest canopy that block light from smaller plants below. For some species there is an ongoing race to gain a permanent place in the sun. Differential rates of growth, based on adaptation to different factors, can determine which individuals and species will survive and how and area will change in the composition of its vegetation.

In other ways the relative rate of growth affects the success of individuals and species. The greater the growth either in spreading leaf crown, root system, or wandering tillers, the more environmental surface there is and the more photosynthesis can be achieved. This means more photosynthates that can be produces and stored to be used either to increase reproduction or survive adverse conditions.

Make careful note of the growth habit of the species in question and of how this may change, if at all, as the plant matures.. One of the first things to note is the pattern of leaf arrangement, or *phyllotaxis*, on the stem. There are a variety of patterns that are species-typical. The leaves are arranged on the stem so that exposure to light is good. Different patterns may coexist in the same habitat, so it is not a question of a particular pattern being more ideal than another in any given locale.

Phyllotaxis is usually recorded as a fraction. Choose a leaf on a stem and then count the number of leaves upward until you come to the leaf directly above the one with which you began. This number will be the lower figure in your fractional notation. You will have spiraled around the stem one or more times in the counting process. Record the number of time you circum-navigated the stem and use it as the upper figure in the fraction. Thus, on a sugar maple, with its opposite leaves, you will go up two leaves to get to the one directly above you starting point and will have gone once around the stem—a one-half phyllotaxy. There are other plants with two-thirds phyllotaxy and three-fifths phyllotaxy. There are other patterns as well, but they are less common.

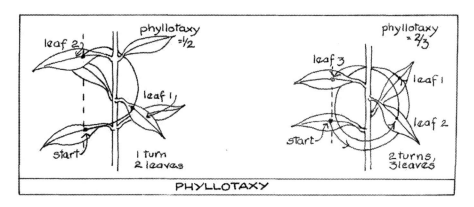

Figure 2-13

Mathematicians have noted that all the patterns fall into a distinctive mathematical series originally described by Fibonnacci and known as the Fibonnacci number or sequence. In that series each succeeding fraction is composed by adding he numerators and denominators of the previous two fraction in the series (i.e. 1/2, 2/3, 3/5, 5/8, 8/13…). Scientist have yet to determine how or why this mathematical precision is built into the development of a plant. However, in recording information for a portrait of any given species you should record its phyllotaxy

Noting phyllotaxy will indirectly lead to observations on growth habit. For some nonwoody (*herbaceous*) plants, the shoot grows only apically and any lateral growth is due to different sizes of leaves. In other species, the stem grows to a given height and is topped with an apical crown of leaves. Flowers are generally borne on a separate flower stalk. Many herbaceous plants show very specific pattern of branching that begin from buds formed in the leaf axils or at the apex of a stem or branch. Much of the form or growth habit of a plant is determined by the angle at which branches diverge from the stem and the distance between branches. The angle can be determined by the use of a simple protractor. Rake a number of readings, average them, and note that the angles of the branches nearest the stem or trunk may differ considerably from those nearer the tips of the branches.

Another factor that affects shape and growth habit is the shade-tolerance of individual leaves. If they cannot tolerate shade, lower leaves and subsequently branches may die and get broken off, thus altering the plant's shape. Because of this, individuals growing close together may have a very different, narrower growth habit from individuals of the species growing by themselves in the open. These plant's shapes may be wide-spreading with branches quite near the ground. Other adverse conditions, such as the drying effect of winds on mountaintop dwellers and salty winds along coast may cause changes in growth habit.

There is a wide diversity to growth patterns. There are those whose stems are not upright but run along the surface of the ground with some species even putting down roots at various points along the stem. Such stems are runners, or *stolons*, and are typical of such species as strawberries. Then there are climbing stems that twist around nearby uprights on the way up or attach to these uprights using coiling tendrils, or suckers. There are species that send up multiple shoots from a common growth point, creating shrubby or bush forms; and there are the grasses that add new growth at their bases or near joints part way up their stems rather than at the tip. Many aquatic species have radically different leaves underwater than those above water. Aside from their intrinsic interest these various growth habits represent strategies for survival and various adaptations for securing resources for life from different environments. Artists as well as scientists revel in the diversity of plant forms.

Botanists recognize true stems by their microscopic anatomy and using that knowledge the have discovered that a number of underground structures that might offhandedly appear to be roots are actually modified stems. *Rhizomes* are a common example. Found on such plants as bracken fern, Solomon's seal, cattails, water-lilies and flags, rhizomes have many buds. In *mono-podial rhizomes* the terminal bud extends the rhizome horizontally from year to year. Side buds grow up to form the above ground leaves and fruiting bodies. Other species have *sym-podial rhizomes* in which the side bud develops a new section of rhizome that will produce a new terminal bud. Bracken has mono-podial rhizomes; Solomon's seal sym-podial ones.

Some underground stems form enlargements called *tubers* that are highly adapted for food storage. The common potato is a good example of a tuber. Tubers are also found on such wild plants as groundnut and arrowhead. *Corms* are short, thickened underground stems. Leaves and flower stalks emerge from the top of the corm; roots below. The food from the leaves is sent below ground to form a new corm just above the old one. You might thing that corms would eventually get closer and closer to the surface as the years pass, but contractile action of the roots keeps pulling the new corms down into the ground to an appropriate level. A number of spring wildflowers like Dutchman's breeches, squirrel corn, and spring beauty have corms. *Bulbs* are very similar and are underground buds usually surrounded by leaf-like structures.

Particularly in arid region where the surface leaves may provide too much water loss for survival, there are plants in which the whole process of photosynthesis goes on in the stem. The leaves, if they exist, are ephemeral or modified into protective devices such as thorns. In such cases, as with cacti and euphorbias, the stem tends to be thick, succulent, and green

THE ROOT OF THE MATTER

Recall that the plumule that grew upward from the expanding seed developed into stem and leaves, and that there also was a radicle that grew downward. The radicle becomes the primary root that will develop into complex root system of the plant. Most plant observers overlook the root system because it is hidden from view. Nonetheless, it is important to become familiar with it for it plays a critical role in the life of vascular plants and is often a key to long-term survival in harsh environments.

Roots have diverse functions. They may provide general or specialized support, absorb water and nutrients, store food manufactured in the leaves, or a combination of these functions. The serious plant observer will take time to examine how a plant's root system is distributed in space. After all half a plants being exists below ground. *How far down do the roots penetrate? How far out from the stem do they spread? How far down does a root go before side roots, if any, branch out?* Two different species may appear to be occupying very similar above ground space but may actually be occupying quite different underground space. For example, in a lawn the grass has shallow, spreading roots while dandelions in the lawn have deep taproots that reach down to a depth of four to six inches. During dry periods, the grass quickly exhausts the near-surface moisture but the dandelion has access to deeper soil moisture and can remain active longer.

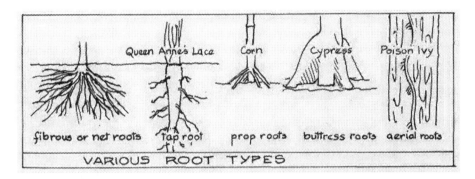

Figure 14

Developing an accurate picture of a root system involves far more work than just pulling a plant from the ground and looking at its roots. For some shallower-rooted species, it can involve digging a trench in one plane and photographing or sketching the roots as they are uncovered. A fire-fighters back pump and a spray mister can be used to jet-wash soil from around the roots. In some cases the plant can be dug out in a large ball of soil. Then you will have to carefully rinse the soil away to reveal the root system.

In prairie and desert soils, or in the case of some trees, the root penetration is so deep that only determination and mechanized digging equipment will permit a thorough mapping of the root system. For some trees the occasional blow-down or erosion along a stream bank will give a fortuitous glimpse of the root system.

If a plant species grows in a variety of habitats, check the pattern of root growth in each different one. You may discover somewhat different patterns adapting the roots to the conditions.

When checking on the root systems, use you hand lens and see if the finer roots are covered with a whitish fungal growth. This most likely would be one of the species of myco-rrhizal fungi that aid the root to be water and minerals from the soil in exchange for some of the photo-synthates stored in the root. Also be alert for small swellings on the roots of such plants as clovers. These house nitrogen-fixing bacteria that also help put nitrates into the soil.

You can also note some of the ways roots respond to the underground world. *What do they do when they encounter a rock of root of an adjacent plant? Can you find places where roots rubbing together have grafted together? Where the roots have developed a corky bark, how far along the root system does the bark extend?*

Not all roots develop below ground. Some species develop adventitious roots at nodes along the stem. Most frequently these adventitious roots are needed primarily for support. Those who have grown corn are familiar with such prop roots at the base of the stalk. In the tropics the screw pine (*Pandanus*) tree is a good example of a plant with prop roots as are the various species of mangrove. Other species that develop aerial roots that grow downward from the crown of the plant, such as the Banyan tree. In Hawaii the ohia trees are often buried in volcanic ash, and in such cases they may develop clusters or aerial root in the crown to take moisture from the clouds that regularly engulf them. The seemingly ubiquitous poison ivy is known for the adventitious roots along its stem that probe dark crevices in bark and help the stem become a climbing vine under certain conditions. When the leaves have fallen, this pattern of adventitious roots lets those "in the know" recognize it from similar climbers such as woodbine or Virginia creeper.

There are tree species in which there is thickening and vertical extension of tissue from the base of the stem out along the roots to form *buttresses*. These buttress roots appear to give the tree greater support from the forces of the wind. The "knees" on cypress trees are another strange root formation. These are upward extensions from the roots that grow above the surface of the swampy waters in which the cypress trees live. The function of these "knees" is not completely clear, but it has long been assumed that they help the roots breathe.

Competition for root space is strong. Where intake of water and nutrients are the primary root functions, the plant extends it roots as rapidly as possible to maximize its control of the local resources in the soil. Dominance by the roots of one species may quite successfully prevent the establishment of the young of another species, or even the young of its own species. The roots of some species, such as many goldenrods, exude chemicals that deter the growth of other plants.

Just as aboveground portions of a tree have their enemies, so do the roots. Check them for insects such as the larvae of beetles and cicadas, nematode worms, and others. Heavy infestation may effectively prune the roots and limit the size of the stems and leaves they can support.

THE LIMITS TO LIFE

With most higher animals, we perceive decline and death to occur to the whole organism at once. This is only an illusion, because different organs tend to age at different rates and death of all the body cells actually occurs over a period of hours. Differential aging of the various parts is generally more apparent with plants, particularly perennials. The plant observer gathering life history material will note the time when different flower parts first appear and when they are shed. Note when individual leaves first appear and how long they live before they yellow, shrivel, and drop off the plant. As one keeps track of a number of leaves on a plant, some indication may be found as to whether the life span of a leaf seems to be guided by some internal clock or by factors that are environmentally determined. This is more of an issue in tropical and subtropical plants, as well as among evergreen species in temperate climates.

In temperate climates the perennial deciduous species build up a corky layer at the base of their leaves that seals off the tubular plumbing systems of the plant (the *xylem* and *phloem* tissues) effectively sealing the doom of the leaf for that season. That corky layer is known as the cutting-off or *abcission* layer and it creates a distinctive scar when the leaf falls off. The chemicals trapped in the withering leaf undergo a variety of changes that provide the sequence of colors of the dying foliage. Since the percentages of these chemicals and their mix tend to vary with the species, it is not surprising that the colors do as well. A careful observer will be able to identify many species of trees and shrubs at a distance by the subtle differences in the foliage colors as the green chlorophyll of summer fades: the bronzy-purple hue of white ash, the deep red or yellow of the red maples, the orange-red and yellow of sugar maples, or the bright yellows of birch and aspen.

If there is annual or seasonal dieback of parts of a plant, keep track of the normal amount. *Is it just the most recent succulent growth? The leaves only? The stem back to the ground? Or back to the transition zone between stem and root, wherever that may be? The grasses and other plants of prairies and marshes also have their distinctive colors as the leaves and stems die back to the roots*

Do not neglect what is happening underground. Often under ground parts also regularly die back, leaving only a tuber or apical growth buds to regenerate new life. If you carefully map the location of some plants year after year, you may get the impression that a plant is slowly marching away from the point where you first spotted it. Indeed it may be, as the previous year's growth dies away and the next year's plant emerges at its side or tip.

You will want to keep track of the life span of the various species you are studying. For the annuals and biennial this is generally easy, but don't take these categories for granted. Biennials growing in poor habitats may live in the rosette stage for more than one year. They keep accumulating food in their roots until they have a sufficient supply to generate a flowering and fruiting stalk. For annuals and biennials the flowering/fruiting process is usually the death knell for the plant. Having expended most of its accumulated photosynthates once the fruits are made, the plant loses vigor, becomes senescent, and dies.

With perennial species, determine the life span is less simple. Some are virtually immortal; many, although long-lived, begin to show a gradual loss of vigor and die. It is hard to think of small plants living so long. I have a red trillium (*Trillium erectum*), or wake robin that I collected from the wild as a teenager over 55 years ago. It has been transplanted to two different homes yet it continues to thrive. There is no way of knowing how old it was when I collected it, and it will probably outlive me!

You will also want to keep track of the mortality factors affecting mature plants. Frequently these may be insects or disease but also may be changing light, temperature, or moisture conditions, or nutritional depletion from the competition from other plant species. Gathering such information will be a slow process based on many observation and notes kept in you journal over an extended period of time.

As individual plants age you may notice a decline in their rate of growth, amount of growth, and reproductive ability as indicated by frequency of flowering and amount of flowers produced. Such information helps round out the picture of the life stages of that species.

PLANT BEHAVIOR

Plants may lack the nervous systems of animal and remain relatively stationary throughout their adult lives, but they are nonetheless sentient—that is, the are perceptive of some aspects of their surroundings. The mechanism for perceiving and responding seems largely to be different from those of most animals, but they do function. The careful and persistent plant observer will note these actions even if their meaning is not immediately clear.

Many species orient their leaves toward or away from the sun throughout the day. *What is the pattern and time sequence? How is it affected by overcast days?* Use your hand lens to check the donut-shaped cells, the *stomates*, on the underside of the leaf. *Is there any correlation between the leaf orientation and whether the stomates generally are open or closed?* Many flowers also follow the sun.

What happens to the leaves at night? Some keep their daytime positions, while other take on a new attitude. That new attitude sometimes referred to as a sleep position.

Stems may also show a definite growth movement toward light and thus affect the growth patterns of the total plant. A plant that gets pushed over may show a sharp bend as their growing point orients toward the light or away from the Earth's gravity. Depending upon the direction of the response, it is referred to as positive (toward) or negative (away). Different parts of the same plant may respond oppositely to the same stimulus. For example, the plumule of many seeds is negatively geotropic while the radical positively geotropic.

Most stems are *negatively geotropic,* growing away from gravity's pull even in darkness. Roots are generally *positively geotropic;* growing downward toward the earth, but study of root systems shows that this is not universally the case. Many grow underground, parallel to the surface of the soil, apparently reacting more negatively to light than positively to gravitational forces.

If a plant has tendrils or a swinging stem for climbing, be alert for *thigmotropism,* the phenomenon of response to touch. The tendrils grow out and wave about, but if the make contact with something they quickly begin to spiral about and grasp the object they have touched. In some plants, the tendril may even shrink once the spiral has been completed, thus pulling the plant closer to its newfound support. Such thigmo-tropic behavior is characteristic of some adventitious roots as well, like those of poison ivy.

The leaflets of mimosa plant show a rapid response to touch by quickly drooping together. The traps of some insect-eating plants also are activated by touch, for example, the Venus-flytrap, and some soil fungi create loops to snare nematode worms.

Many plants respond to water. It's common to speak of roots following water gradients in the soil as hydrotropism, but evidence for such is very slim and shaky. Some trees, however, like elms, willows, and poplars have a propensity for finding crack in water pipes and entering them with their roots. On the other hand, rapid changes in internal water pressure, or *turgor*, account for the mechanism of a number of plant movements such as the opening and closing of the breathing pores (stomates) and the sleep movements of leaves. Some grasses, such as beach grass, have grooved leaves with cells that may lose water and shrink during drought. This results in the leaf curling into a tube to help prevent further water loss through transpiration.

On a different time scale, the plant observer should be alert for evidence of *co-evolution*, the adaptation of plants to interaction with animals. Sometimes this evidence is relatively simple to find, such as the development of protective thorns or spines or the production of toxic chemicals as defense weapons against excessive predation by animals. In other cases, it is much more complex and involves modifications for pollination by specific animal groups or even species, such as bats, butterflies, moths, and bees. There are also defense mechanisms whereby certain insects such as ants or wasps are attracted and accommodated with benefit to them that such mechanisms, thorns and the like, provide effective deterrent action against browsing creatures. Such complex co-evolutionary developments are more common in tropical and subtropical regions. The development of partnership between mycor-rhizal fungi and some plant roots is yet another example of co-evolutionary behavior. The relationships develop and generally become refined as the increase benefits to the participants, resulting in some survival advantage over others of their kind.

What you will want to note is what other species regularly attempt to interact with a plant in a co-action, and how the plant responds to the attention—i.e. by chemical or mechanical repellants, attractant, or toleration. Note also what adaptation the animals have for responding positively to the attractants or for circumventing the repellants.

We have implied that there are two major categories of plant behavior: (1) responsive, as in the case of tropisms, and (2) adaptive as in the case of protective and attractant devices. Another form of adaptive behavior to note is the mechanisms for expanding the population of the species. These mechanisms are discussed in the section reproduction, but the alert observer will be looking at not only the simple mechanism but at how that mechanism creates a strategy for perpetuating and expanding the population of a species as well as how the individual plant reproduces. We will discuss the nature of various strategies and the investigation more fully in an upcoming chapter.

GENERAL INFORMATION

There are a number of odds and ends to be noted about a plant to round out its life history and compose a more complete description of the species. Some are related to individuals of the species, other to the local population of the species and other species with which it associates.

Resistance to environmental stress. Plants face a variety of stresses from the physical and biological environment. Determine and not such things a resistance to drought, flooding, burial in sand or mud, intense cold, frost, water-table fluctuations, salinity (from road salting as well as coastal or arid-land salinity), fires, ice, grazing trampling, and similar phenomena. Don't forget the impact of human activities such as logging, tilling, herbiciding, and many others.

Population Data. *What is the average number of individuals per unit area for the species in your region? Does any particular age or size class dominate in your area of study? Does the population appear to be stable or is it increasing or declining?* Again we will discuss methods for determining such information in a later in Appendix D.

Species Associates. *What other species are usually present in the same general area as you study species? Are there some that are always present with your species of interest? A re the species that tend to appear when populations of the study species begin to decline?* Species are usually found in association with other plants and more information on this can be found in Chapter 5.

Variability. A major effect of sexual reproduction is to produce variability. Much of the variability will never be expressed in a mature plant: the genetic alteration is non-adaptive at the moment. It seems to be a very wasteful lifestyle, yet if condition change slightly there is a chance that one of the variants may be suited to the change and will survive to pass along its uniqueness to the following generations. In addition a number of variations are produced and survive because they are not maladaptive—that is, they do not seriously affect the plant in any negative way. These we search for among a population of plants. Some species seem quite plastic and produce a large number of subtle variants that show a mall degree of variation. These latter species will probably be most vulnerable to environmental alteration by humans or nature. Populations developed vegetatively, in particular, show low variability and thus a high degree of vulnerability to environmental changes.

Habitat Preferences. Once a plant sprouts from its seed coat and sends down its radicle, it is locked into a site. It can't decide it doesn't like it there and get up and move elsewhere. Either the habitat is right and the young plant becomes established and thrives, or it dies. Depending upon the degree of suitability of the site, the death can come swiftly or longer over a period of tame as the too-limited resources are gradually exhausted or competition for them becomes excessive.

You will want to note man things about the sites where a species is growing successful and also about those where it grows with obvious lack of vigor. What are the characteristic of the soil, its texture, nutrients, depth, erodability, and the like? What is the pH of the soil? What is its water holding characteristics? What kind of microclimate exists where the species grows—that is, what is the surrounding vegetation, slope, exposure, altitude, or other factors affecting insulation, wind, heat and moisture? What are the general stresses of the habitat, such as recurring flooding, persistent wind, periodic fire or erosive forces? Gathering aspects of such information is to be explored later on in Chapter 4.

FOR EVERYTHING THERE IS A SEASON

In building an account of a species, we want to build a chronology of the events in the plant's life, particularly the recurring season events such as the appearance of seedling, first leaves, flowers, shedding of pollen, ripening of fruit, and dropping of leaves. We may be able to correlate such events with environmental conditions as day length, rainfall patterns, and temperature averages. The science of such seasonal events is known as *phenology*. It is a particularly rewarding activity for the dedicated amateur plant observer. The beginning phenologist usually notes only the big, obvious events such as the date the first blossom of a species appears, but once hooked he or she begins to elaborate more fully, noting not only first and lasts but when the bulk of the local population is blooming and records of other events.

With each species be sure to keep a record of what months some part of the plant is observable above ground and note the gross changes you see. For example, many weeds are visible all winter if you can recognize the forms of their dried stalks, rosettes of basal leaves, and/or seedpods. Such materials look quite different from the more vibrant living stems and leaves—different but still beautiful.

Phenological records can be kept in charts such as those illustrated in Figure x or on regular calendars from year to year. Reflecting on several years' data may indicate whether certain recurring events are more under the control of some form of internal clock or are more variable and responsive to weather conditions. More detail of procedures for keeping phenological records is presented in Chapter 6.

SUMMARY

In this chapter we have suggested many of the questions to be asked about a plant species if you truly want to know it. Most of the question can be answered about the species by patient and persistent observation. Some answers will be found reasonably quickly; others will emerge only after many years and an occasional bit of luck. Plant observing is an activity for a lifetime, actually several lifetimes. No matter where you are or what season of the year, there are plant observations to be made. For the avid pant observer, time seldom weighs heavy on the mind. And of course there are many more questions that have been set forth here that might be asked. As you become more deeply involved, these will come to you ans you Will seek their answers

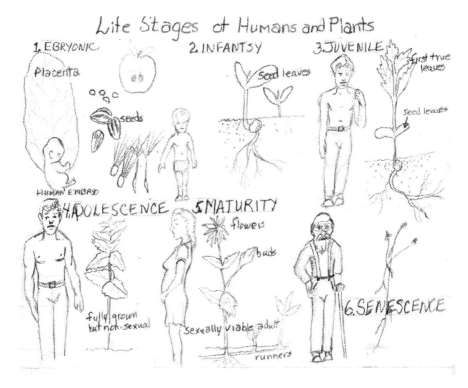

Figure 2-15

3

CONVENTIONAL AND SCIENTIFIC CONCEPTS OF PLANTS

Botanist Ruth Davis suggested that "to many people green stuff is green stuff." Of course that is not the case at all an, indeed, today all "green stuff is not even regarded as being true plant life. Not many years ago, anything living that was not an animal was considered to be a plant. Further elaboration suggested that plant cells had stiff walls to bound them, while animal cells were bounded only by more flexible cell membranes. Only plants contained the green pigment chlorophyll that permitted them to trap energy from the sun. As a group, the fungi created some problems of classification. Although they had cell walls like those of plants, they lacked chlorophyll. They were nonetheless considered to be plants. There were also some one-celled organisms with cell membranes like and animal but with chlorophyll like a plant. Zoologists claimed they were animals; botanists encompassed them as plants.

In the past few decades those people who spend their lives trying to arrange living things into groupings that indicate some sort of evolutionary relationships have decided that living thing represent not two major division, or kingdoms (plant and animal), but rather at least five major kingdoms. Not all taxonomists agree, but today the most widely accepted classification system recognizes the kingdoms Monera, Protoctista, Fungi, Plantae, and Animalia. *Monera* includes single-celled organisms in which the nuclear material is not bounded by a nuclear membrane. This group encompasses the various kinds of bacteria and blue-green algae. *Protoctista* have cells in which the nuclear material is enclosed in a nuclear membrane. Most are single-celled, but there are a number of multi-cellular forms including the seaweeds. This kingdom includes nucleated algae, water molds, slime molds, and the protozoa. *Fungi* are also organisms with nucleated cell, but all species lack chlorophyll and reproduce sexually by spores. Fungi include molds, mushrooms, and mycorrhizal fungi. *Animalia* are multi-cellular creatures that, after fertilization, develop from a hollow ball of cells called a *blastula*. They are unable to capture energy directly from the sun but get directly or indirectly from autotrophic plants. Plantae are multi-cellular organisms with some form of vascular system that reproduce sexually and contain chloroplasts.

You can see that many of the organisms most people would call plants are now scattered over three kingdoms, or four—if you think of bacteria as plants. Many of these organisms are small and require considerable technical expertise and equipment for their study. However in each kingdom, with the possible exception of Monera, there are large conspicuous groups that the alert amateur is likely to encounter and be curious about. In this volume I have chosen to discuss the organisms from the kingdoms Plantae and Protoctista, because the average person will continue to think of these organisms as plants.

HERBACEOUS PLANTS

Non-woody, flowering land plants are those that generally come to mind when people talk about herbaceous plants. These are the wildflowers, grasses, cacti, and other succulents that attract wildflower buffs. Many of these kinds of plants have been transformed by selection and breeding into our garden and house plants. For most plant watchers these are the kinds of plants that first demand our attention.

In this book we tend to downplay flower listing, but it can be a thoroughly enjoyable activity when you are on vacation or a business trip and builds a general familiarity with the flora of an unfamiliar region. In fact, it is fun to schedule trips to desert, prairie, and mountainous regions during the peak of their bloom periods just for the sheer visual delight of it.

In the United States and Canada it is possible to acquire relatively inexpensive local identification guides to the most common flowers at gift shops and visitor cents of most national parks. These booklets generally are useful for a much broader geographical area than just the designated park. Often there are several different booklets available; look over each one carefully before buying it Try to get as many well-illustrated species as possible for you money. Most of these small guides also point you in the direction of the most authoritative references for the region so that if necessary you can dig deeper later.

These guidebooks can also be used as a checklist on your trip. I usually put a checkmark in the margin next to each species sighted, along with the date it was first observed and where. On a recent trip through the northern Rockies, for instance, my wife and I ticked off 85 of the 125 plants listed in the little guidebook we had bought and we also noted a number of other species not included in that book but identified elsewhere. It wasn't the kind of record one would keep for a real exploration of that flora, but it was a pleasant enrichment of what was fundamentally a wildlife photography trip.

Don't hesitate to make sketches and color notes of unidentifiable (from your particular guidebook) flowers. Take the sketches t o park naturalists who can help you with at least tentative identification. A set of colored pencils is helpful for such sketching. Be sure to represent leaf shape and positioning on the plant as accurately as possible and also individual flower shape and arrangement of flower clusters. The more detail and accuracy in your sketch, the greater the likelihood that the ranger/naturalist can positively identify it or that you can work it through more technical plant keys later.

FERNS AND THEIR ALLIES

Herbaceous plants in general have a vascular system for transporting food and water among the living cells, and are capable of reproducing through seeds. Seeds have a tough outer coating surrounding an embryonic plant.

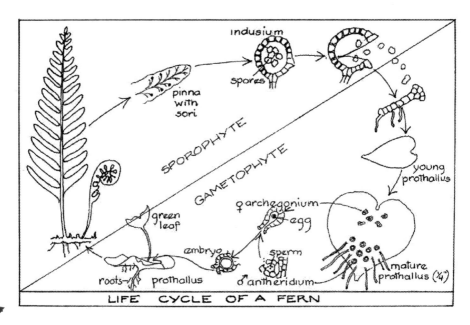

Figure 3-1

Ferns and their allies are similar to the herbaceous plants in having a vascular system; however, instead of seed they reproduce from spores. Spores do not contain an embryo and the cellular structure that grows from them has in each cell only half the normal number of chromosomes to be found in the mature fern plant. Fern spores develop into a thin, flat, ribbon like structure known as a *prothalium*. A prothallium develops two small structure on its lower surface; one is shaped like a little upside-down flask and is known as an *archegonium*, containing an egg cell, while the other kind of structure, an *antheridium*, appears like a little pimple. Inside the antheridium are spiral-shaped male cells which botanists call *antherozoids*. The underside of a prothallium also has a number of thread-like structures that help hold the plant in place. Unlike roots, these *rhizoids* have no vascular structure.

If a small film of water is present, antherozoids can swim to the eggs and one will fuse with an egg forming a structure with the normal (diploid) number of chromosomes, called a *zygote*. This is a sexual union. A zygote will go through a series of cell divisions that will produce leaves, called *fronds*, that we recognize as being ferns. In due time some fronds develop structures that produce new spores.

Notice that in a fern life cycle there are two kinds of fern plants: a prothallium that develops asexually from a spore, and fern fronds that develop from a sexually produced zygote generated by the prothallium stage. This alternation between asexual and sexual development stages is the phenomenon known as alternation of generations. Ferns and fern allies are not totally restricted to reproducing through this process. In some species there are forms of vegetative reproduction,

Although ferns are widespread in tropical regions, they can be found in almost every habitat except the most arid. There are even a few truly aquatic species, such as *Marsilia*, which resembles and underwater four-leaf clover. Ferns tend to have rather specific habitat requirements and the plant observer needs to take careful note of the physical conditions where each species is found. Some, of course, show a broader range of tolerance than others.

Forms of fern growth are worth noting. Some species send up their fronds from around a vertical stem, or rootstalk, and the leaves tend to create a graceful crown. With such species, new fronds appear at the outside of the rootstalk so that each year a circle of fronds gets somewhat larger. With evergreen species you may find a circle of winter-flattened, green leaves on the ground with a new circle of coiled fronds, or *crosiers* (sometimes called fiddleheads),poking up through. Other species have a horizontal stem, or *rhizome*, that lies on or just under the surface. New growth emerges from the tip of the rhizome. A rhizome will continue to grow for years, sending down new roots near the fronds and often slowly decaying moving a fair distance from its original germination spot.

Ferns are handsome plants that are fun, though often frustrating to identify. Fortunately there are fewer species to master than among seed plants. Identification of many ferns is possible based on growth habit, habitat and similar factors, but positive identification of confusing species depends upon close examination of the spore-bearing structures. You will need a good hand lens for much of that. Most ferns bear their spores on the underside of some or all of the leaflets (*pinnules*) of the frond, but there are species that produce separate fronds devoted solely to producing spores. Fronts that produce spores are known *as fertile fronds,* other are called *sterile fronds.*

On a typical fertile frond you will find bundles of sporangia, or *sori.* Often a sorus is covered with a flap or umbrella-like lid known as an *indusium.* The indusium may be attached to the sorus at its edge or in the middle. There are round indusia, curved indusia, long and narrow indusia, and absent indusia. The presence or absence of an indusium, its method of attachment, shape and spacing are specific for each species of fern. The language of fern parts seems confusing and awkward at first, but with persistence it won't be long before you grasp it and use it to begin unraveling the mysteries of which fern is which.

You can then begin to gather some phenological information about local ferns. When do the croziers first appear? How long does it take for the average crozier to fully uncoil? How long does it take for the frond to reach full size? How long does the average frond survive? How many fronds does a plant put up in a season? When do sori begin to appear? Do all fronds become fertile? If not, is it younger or older fronds that become fertile? When do fronds die back?

There are also a great many questions to explore about a species' preferences, tolerances, and habits. What are its soil and light requirements? How long do individual plants live? Is the species a competitor or a stress—tolerator (see Chapter) How rapidly, and in what fashion, does a colony establish itself and expand? Do the individual plants, move about? If so, at what annual rate? Is there evidence of any individuals actually moving out of a good habitat? What animal life feeds on ferns? Are there species of animals associated closely with ferns in any other way (i.e. hummingbirds use cinnamon fern fuzz to line nests)? Can you locate any prothallia in the area? If so, under what condition have t he spores germinated and survived? How near is the nearest spore-bearing fern to this prothallium? How do the adult ferns weather periodic drought?

Even though the variety of species is relatively small compared to seed plants, there is a great diversity among ferns. There are tree ferns in the tropics, and tree-dwelling epiphytes as well. There are climbing ferns; ferns with strap-shaped leaves, that root at their tips, and both emergent and submergent species of water-dwelling ferns. Such beauty and diversity has attracted many people to an interest in fern both in the wild and as captives in garden, green-house, and dwelling.

Growing Prothallia

Because people are usually more familiar with seeds and seedlings, you are urged to broaden your experience by trying your hand at growing some spores to produce prothallia. Indeed, you may want to attempt growing as many different fern species from spores and develop a photographic record of their prothallia and the first you fronds that arise from them. Growing ferns from spores is not particularly difficult, but it does take time and patience. On average it takes six to ten months from the time of sowing spores until young ferns are large enough to be transplanted.

Several methods can be used, but for a beginner the inverted pot method is probably most satisfactory. Take a clean, porous, clay flowerpot, one not too large to be completely covered with a glass jar. Fill the pot with sphagnum or peat moss, then invert it in a shallow dish or saucer. Pour boiling water over the pot and saucer several times to sterilize them. Drain and cool. Sprinkle the spores over the surface of the inverted pot and then cover it with a glass jar. Place water in the saucer from time to time as needed.

Collect spores when sporangia are light brown and the indusia are still intact. Green indusia indicate that the spores are not yet ripe; frayed and/or shriveled sporangia indicate that the spores have already been shed. Put the fronds, with sporangia down, on paper. Cover with a jar to keep the spores from blowing away. In a day or so carefully remove the fronds from the paper, leaving behind as little else as possible besides spores. Replace the jar and avoid drafts while carefully moving the paper and jar to your sterilized pot. Tap the spores of the paper onto the clay pot.

After sowing the spores, place the flowerpot and glass jar setup in filtered sunlight of low to medium intensity, or under a fluorescent lamp where it can receive eight to sixteen hours of light per day. Temperatures between 680F and 860F are best Water when necessary, preferably with cooled, boiled water or distilled water. Weak solutions of liquid fertilizer can be added to the water every couple of weeks after a green mat of prothallia appears

Once the mat of prothallia has formed, you can transplant 1/4 inch pieces of the material onto the surface of a planting medium (for instance, sphagnum peat) in a clear plastic container with a lid. Place pieces about 1/2 inch apart. The planting medium should be sterilized, disinfected and drenched with fungicide before being used with the prothallia. Press prothallia clumps firmly onto the medium and mist them with distilled water. Cover and continue to observe. As young fern fronds begin to grow, you may want to divide the again. In time you can remove the cover and let the young fronds toughen. They can then be transplanted to individual peat posts for eventual transfer outdoors or to indoor or patio planters.>

Fern Allies

Like ferns, the fern allies—clubmosses, quillworts, and selaginellas—reproduce by spores, although there are anatomical differences in the spore-bearing structures. It was once believed that these groups of plats were closely related to ferns, but more recent studies indicate a more distant relationship. We are still much about them, for they have not received as much attention as ferns.

It seems strange that the existence of spores was not discovered until 1669 although seeds and their purpose have been well known since the dawn of humankind. It wasn't until 1848 that science learned how spores grew into fern plants. Remarkably, there are still fern allies who have not had their life cycle completely documented. Unfortunately, many of them do not respond as readily as ferns to laboratory or home propagation.

Most diverse in form of the fern allies are the clubmosses, or *lycopodiums*. In ages past, ancestors of today's species included some rather large, treelike species, although today's species are all comparatively small. Clubmosses do have some moss-like qualities to their appearance, but because they have a vascular system to distribute food and water, they are able to be larger than true mosses. Many species resemble four-to-six inch high evergreen trees, a characteristic that is reflected in such common names as "ground pine" and "running pine."

Lycopodiums tend to spread by creeping stems that send down roots at intervals and send up evergreen shoots. It is on the shoots that the reproductive organs are born. In most clubmosses this is a cone-shaped structure called a *strobilus*. There are species, however, like shining clubmoss *(Lycopodium lucidulum)* that have pinhead-sized spore-bearing sacs in the axils of the upper leaves instead of a strobilus.

Exploring life cycles of clubmosses takes considerable time, patience, and luck. The small percentage of the millions of spores produced that do germinate tend to do so beneath the soil surface. Researchers believe that it may take clubmoss spores as long as seven years to develop into a prothallium and another decade for that structure to send a new clubmoss shoot above the ground! It us little wonder that clubmosses are only poorly known at present.

Existence for a clubmoss is a constant race between life and death. It grows from new shoots at the stem tips while dying back at the other end. It must be able to provide new growth at least as fast as it decays. In many area, clubmosses have suffered greatly from over-collection for Christmas wreaths and terraria. This is unfortunate since their slow development means they re-colonize and area very, slowly if at all. What's more, they are generally unsuited to terraria and wild gardens for which they are collected because they do not transplant readily.

You may find it informative to tie markers loosely at the growing points of some plants and keep track of the rate of growth of individuals along with their accompanying rate of decay.

Horsetail and scouring rushes are another group of fern allies. Fertile fronds of horsetails look as though they were designed by a Middle Eastern religious architect since they are composed of tiers of crown-like scales at each stem joint pile one atop the other, culminating in a club-shaped minaret which is the strobilus. Sterile fronds follow the same stem pattern, but branches at the joints grow out into green stringy leaflets that give the plant a bush appearance suggestive of the tail of a green horse! If you keep phenological records of these plants you will note that their fertile fronds appear very early and die back by summer. So different are the fertile and sterile frond of some species, it would be easy for the uninitiated to believe they were dealing with two distinct species on the same site. Scouring rushes are green and manufacture food in the stem. The hollow stalks, which are beautifully banded in black and white at each joint, also contain grains of silica, the mineral of most sands. Because of this, people have long used the stalks to scour pans and the like, thus the name. Unlike horsetail, scouring rushes do not have fertile and sterile forms, but produce strobili at the tips of the food-producing stalks.

Look for the horsetail tribe in wet meadows, along stream banks, and in disturbed, loose, sandy-gravelly, wet soils such as railway embankments and roadsides. There are a number of species of horsetails *(Equisetum)* to be found in temperate zones. One must be careful in identifying them for some, like the common field horsetail (*Equisetum arvense*), have a wide variety of forms of the one species and, unfortunately, these many forms blend with one another creating considerable confusion. Those of you with an ecological bent should examine the locations of the root-stalks in the ground for this varies considerably, affecting the plant's role in its community.

Not to be forgotten among fern allies are quillworts, all of which belong to one genus, *Isoetes*. There are about seventy species world-wide, almost all of them aquatic or semi-aquatic in habit. Quillworts all look similar and prefer similar habitats. They tend to resemble clumps of chives or small onions with a flattened, spoon-shaped base to each leaf. They often grow among similar-appearing aquatic and semi-aquatic grasses so that they get overlooked. As might be expected, quillworts have received relatively little attention from researchers.

Quillworts do have some features that bear attention, however. They have the largest spore cases of any living vascular plants. The spore cases contain two types of the spores: the large female megaspores and tiny male microspores. Sporangia are located in pockets at the base of a corm, and the outer leaves are the oldest; the innermost ones the youngest. In most species young leaves are sterile; the outer most, fertile ones. Sporangia of the outer leaves are filled with megaspores, while the middle, fertile leaves bear microspores in their sporangia. However, there are some species that bear both spore types within one sporangium.

The two different spores both produce prothallia, but microspore prothallia produce only male spermartozoids and macrospore prothallia produce eggs. Young quillwort leaves grow only from macrospore prothallia. Macrospores of quillworts are large enough to be seen by the naked eye, but examination under a binocular microscope reveals a variety of surface textures depending upon the species. The upper segment of each macrospore has three ridges that meet at the apex; a circumferential ridge joins the opposite ends of the ridges. The area between the ridges may be pitted *(reticulate)*, pebbled (*tuberculate*), prickly (*echinate*) or crested (*cristate*), characteristics that are used to make positive identification among quillwort species. Because it is awkward to a carry a binocular microscope into the field, you will have to take home appropriate voucher specimens.

Last of the fern allies are the spikemosses, or *selaginellas*. This not a large group of plants, with only about 800 species worldwide. The creeping, prostrate forms are largely tropical in distribution and prefer moist habitats. The more upright, stiff species are found in drier, rockier areas and are more common outside the tropics. There are only a few dozen species of this group in North America. Like quillworts, selaginellas produce both macro—and micro—spores. Sporangia are born in the axils of the upper leaves. It takes a sharp observer to spot colonies of these plants and a determined one to follow their life histories.

Mosses and Liverworts

Mosses and liverworts form a natural grouping of plants of considerable similarity. Besides being associated together in lay peoples' minds, scientists assemble them all under one plant phylum, *Bryophyta*. Modern bryophytes are all low-growing plants, with most species ranging between 1/16 of an inch to about two inches in height. They all lack roots with a vascular system, having instead only tiny, hair-like rhizoids that anchor the plant to its substrate and absorb a little moisture that must be transmitted directly from cell to cell. Some bryophites are thin, flat, scale-like growths (*thallus plants*) that press close to the substrate, held by the rhizoids on their underside. Most bryophytes do have true stems and leaves with some form of vascular system. Because the do not have roots to bring them water and nutrients, and must take moisture in through the individual cells and pass it from cell to cell, they must either establish themselves in habitats that are perennially moist and/or shielded from solar desiccation, or develop good conservation techniques and capacity to withstand drought while concentrating growth and reproduction during the brief periods of adequate moisture.

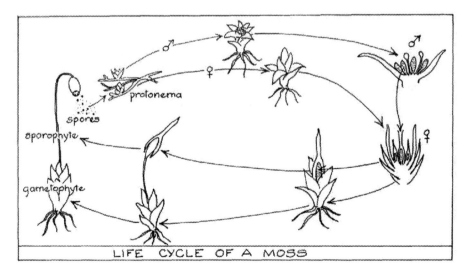

LIFE CYCLE OF A MOSS

Figure 3-2

Bryophytes are all spore-bearing plants exhibiting a pattern of alternation of generations. With brophytes the sexual (*gametophyte*) stage is the dominant one. The asexual (*sporophyte*) generation grows from the gametophyte stage and is partially or totally dependent upon it for its nutrition. Although bryophytes are land plants, with very few exceptions, they undoubtedly evolved from aquatic species. They still depend upon presence of a water film for their mobile sperms to swim to a waiting egg cell.

Mosses are among our most aesthetically pleasing plants, often forming extensive velvety or springy carpets over the ground. During a hike or forest stroll, nothing quite beats a spread-eagled break on a mossy carpet or the joy of shedding shoes and socks to walk barefooted over such a cool, velvety rug. Unfortunately, common usage has bestowed the name moss on a number of non-moss plants such as the tree-dwelling Spanish moss of the south-land (a *bromeliad)*; the 'beard moss" or northern evergreen forests (*Usnea*, a lichen);the "reindeer moss" of the arctic (*Cladonia,* a lichen); or such "flowering mosses" as moss rose, moss pink, and the like (all are flowering plants; no true moss has flowers). Although this is unfortunate, it should not confuse any true moss observer.

The life cycles of bryophytes are observable by those who look close to the ground with a hand lens. Each begins when the single cell of a germinating spore grows into a branching, green, threadlike structure (a *protonema*). Many partitions along the thread are at an angle rather than straight across and some of its branches penetrate into the ground. A protonema may cover several inches, occasionally even several feet, of ground. In due time a bud or buds form on the protonema from which, depending on the species, a thallus or leafy stem will grow. Branches that grew into the soil become rhizoids.

The thallus or leafy plants have only half the normal number of chromosomes. These haploid plants produce the sexual structures. Borne in a cluster of leaves or in a pocket of the thallus, the *antheridia* produce male cells that swim using two hair-like *cilia.* Eggs are borne in the base of a structure, the *archegonium,* which looks like a long-necked vase. When an egg is ripe, its archegonium exudes a sugary or proteinaceous mucilage through the neck of the vase. Male cells are attracted to the mucilage like bees to honey, and they swim to the substance, then down the tube to where one will arrive to fertilize and egg, thy creating a *zygote.*

Zygotes remain in place in their arachegonium and grow into rather strange diploid plants, the sporophytes. Each has a cluster of cells *(foot)* in the base of the archegonium, along with a long, flexible hairlike structure (*seta*), topped off by a capsule in which the spores form. Thus, spore cases are not organs of the basic carpetlike moss plants but are actually sporophytes ridding piggyback on gametophytes. When a seta and capsule push out of an archegonium, they often wear the tip of that structure like a cap. In fact, it is from this hairy, netlike structure that haircap mosses get their name. This cap is called a *calyptera*. Its shape is often a diagnostic feature for identifying certain mosses.

The thallus of a liverwort produces rather strange structures that house antheridia and archegonia. In some species these structures look like umbrellas or flat discs; in other species they are cone-shaped. It is a challenge for male cells from and antheridiaphore to reach an egg in an archegoniaphore, and with many species it is not at all clear how this is accomplished. In any case, one a zygote is formed from the fusion of the two sex cells; it divides to form a sporophyte. Its food embeds in the tissue of the gametophyte and the seta with its capsule for as described above; eventually spores form and are released.

Not all liverworts have a thallus; many have stems and leaves. Three rows of leaves are formed, two rows side by side with the third row on the underside of the other two. These create some beautiful and distinctive patterns. Archegonia form at the tip of stems. At the point where a zygote forms and the sporophyte develops, there usually is a circlet of modified leaves (the *perianth*) surrounding the spore—bearing capsule.

A serious observer, willing to prostrate him—or herself regularly to peer through a magnifying glass, can follow much of the reproductive process and perhaps even note the subtle differences in the process among various species.

Bryophytes, particularly liverworts, have several means of vegetative reproduction in addition to the alternation of generations. Thalli grow and branch at their tips, and the material behind the growth points slowly decays away. As decay works its way to a fork in a thallus, it may cause a separation that results in two plants. Each continues to grow on its own. You can record such development through a photo-sequence of the same area over time. As a frame of reference for relocating a spot, paint a small enamel dot near the plant you are studying; always frame the dot at the same place in your subsequent photographs allowing you better comparison of the changes.

On some thalli you may see little cups about 1/8 inch in diameter. These are called *gemmae cups*, because they hold little flat pieces of thallus tissue called *gemmae*. Splashing water, or raindrops, can wash out these gemmae, each of which is capable or growing into a new liverwort plant. Are you a good enough observer to spot some freshly established gemmae nearby?

There is much phenological information to be gathered about mosses and liverworts. When do sporopytes appear on the plants? How does this correlate with the temperature and rainfall patterns of your area? When do protonemata appear? How long does it take before the start sending up young leafy shoots or thalli? How long-lived are the individual moss plans? How long-lived is the moss bed or colony?

There is also much to explore about bryophtes' environmental needs and their plant associates. You can set up a number of small quadrats for studying bryophytes, carefully mapping distribution of the species and noting the substrates (such as soil, rock, decaying stumps, bark, etc) on which they occur. You can also record pH of the substrate and general moisture regimen of the microclimate, light intensities, and temperature of the microclimate where the particular bryophytes are growing. Are any of the species specific enough in their requirements that they can serve as environmental indicators?

Growing Protonemata

To get a better idea of what protonemata look like so you can more effectively spot them in the wild, you may wish to grow some at home using essentially the same setup as described in the preceding section of the chapter on growing fern prothallia. The only difference is that you substitute moss spores for fern spores and you do not transplant a protonemata. Instead, you leave them on the clay pot.

If you can get clear plastic-lidded boxes about 4"x 8" x2", they also make good rearing boxes for moss protonemata. Put down a 1/2" layer of peat and cover it with a 1/2" layer of sterilized soil. Carefully drench the soil and peat with boiling water; then drain and cool. Spores from a capsule of your moss are then scattered over the surface and the lid is put on. The box is then placed in filtered sunlight at a temperature in the mid-70 degree range. Spores will normally germinate in about two weeks with branched protonemata developing by about four weeks. Once you are familiar with the protonemata, you should search for the in the field, and then note the places and conditions under which they are found.

If you have been successful growing protonemata, you may want to experiment with growing each species on different substrates. Is the nature of the substrate a determining factor in whether or not a spore germinates or a protonema becomes established, producing a thallus or leafy stem.>

Taking Voucher Specimens

Collect some of each moss for identification and voucher specimens, taking about two square inches of a clump. This will allow for breaking of plants when separating them and permit you to maintain some moist and some dry while trying to identify them. Wrap each specimen in a separate paper, mark it with place, date, and habitat, and assign it a collection number. Put all the specimens in a tight plastic or metal box to keep them fresh for several days. Select the best looking, largest, greenest-looking plants, preferably those bearing spore capsules. You can assign to genus and many species without the capsules present, but there are species that cannot be determined accurately without them.>

Other Things to Look for with Bryophytes

Moisture conditions affect behavior of mosses in several ways. Notice the position of leaves in wet and dry weather. How do they differ? Examine closely rip spore capsules with your magnifying glass. If a capsule has a calyptera, remove it gently. The capsule usually has a lid (operculum) which when ripe falls off, revealing a set of fleshy teeth around the opening (peristome from peri=around and stome=opening) During most periods, these peristome teeth fold inward over the opening, holding in the spores. In dry times, they open outward, permitting the spores to float away. Variations in peristome teeth are often identifying characteristics for moss species. Sphagnum mosses are plants of very wet areas such as bogs and marshes, but they need dry periods to disperse their spores. Dryness builds up such tension in the spore cases that they produce a distinctly audible popping sound when they finally rupture. It is a strange experience to sit in sphagnum country at the proper time and listen to these miniature "fireworks" going off about you.

Bryophytes may appear small to us but, relatively, they are giant forests to some animals. Observe the species that associate with the plants. They are invariably so small that you will need your hand lens and perhaps a binocular microscope. There is evidence that several small insects are particularly fond of the mucilage produced by sexual organs of these plants and that these insects play a role in transferring male gametes to eggs. There are also large numbers of strange little animals, like *tardigrades* (so-called water bears) and mites found on many species. Are they feeding on the plants? Do they have some other relationship with them, and if so, what?

The world of bryophytes is wide open for exploration. Although there are not large numbers of people studying the, there are enough to have formed an organization, *The American Bryological and Lichenology Society* (c/o Department of Botany, Southern Illinois University, Carbondale, IL. 62901, which publishes *The Bryologist*, a magazine that is must reading for serious amateurs.

TREES, SHRUBS, AND VINES

All of these are clearly in the modern kingdom Plantae. In large measure they tend to be among the dominant members of their respective communities. Adult trees in general are characterized by a well-defined stem, a diameter at maturity in excess of two inches, and a height over fifteen feet. Trees also have a well-formed crown of branches. By contrast shrubs have a number of stems at or near ground level and usually do not reach the fifteen-foot height, although there are exceptions. As with any attempt to pigeonhole living things, there are always borderline cases, like gray birch (*Betula populifolia*), that demonstrate aspects of both definitions.

Trees and shrubs are woody, with stems essentially erect and self-supporting. Vines, or more properly lianas, do not fully support themselves, but fasten themselves by twisting around a support or grasping to other plants with tendrils or other devices. Some merely trail over others. Liana can be either woody or herbaceous and are found most abundantly in tropical forests.

Largely because of their many uses and height economic importance to humans, trees are among the best known plants. They have not only been carefully examined to determine their potential uses, but their relationships to the physical environment and the impact o each species on other species have been well detailed so that forests can be effectively managed and plantations established for reforestation. Such study is known as *sylvics*. Several good publications detail for each species other trees with which it regularly associate, soil conditions, light preferences, seed production, growth patterns and the like. This does not mean that there is nothing new to be discovered about our trees, only that much less is known about many other kinds of plants.

Trees are good plants for urban plant observers to become involved. Every city has street trees and parks, and some have an arboretum. Such tees comprise the "urban forest." Remove the buildings and you have a forest left behind. You will not be able to see all stages in a tree's life history, because city trees get little chance to reproduce on their own—but there is much else to observe. Urban trees are subject to a number of stresses, some of which are common to normal forest trees. But many of these stresses are unique to the urban scene, such as pavement crowding roots and blocking the soil from soaking up adequate water; shade from tall building; pollution from vehicle exhausts; and road salt. Urban tree watcher can organize a street-tree inventory and keep notes on the health and condition of each tree. Note when trees bloom and produce seed; the time of leafing out; leaf coloration (yellow and brown patches may indicate nutrient or moisture depletion); insect infestation; diseases; and other such information. If a tree appears to be suffering from some, the appropriate official can be notifies and encouraged to take remedial action. A number of cities are even beginning to have urban forester. You should find out if your city has one; if it does, make his or her acquaintance—you probably share a number of common interests. You may want to work with forester in planning and developing expansion of the urban forest and/or replacement of aging or sick members of the present forest.

Tracking the Big Trees

There are a number of interesting projects relating to trees for both urban and rural plant watchers. One involves hunting down the largest specimens of each tree species that grows in your community and recording their location, girth, and height. If you enjoy this, expand your territory by looking for the biggest specimens that still exist in your county and/or state, In your searches you will discover a variety of interesting places; some will be very wild places, others quite civilized. Many of these giant trees represent a long history and deserve some protection to let them persist in our modern world. Your list of the biggest and their challengers will help indicate areas that deserve attempts at preservation or other types of protection.

At a national level, the American Forestry Association has maintained since 1940 a National Register of Big Trees. As time passes, old champions die or are destroyed and their ranking must be taken over by one of the challengers. These may reside in the same state as the former champion or be elevated from a state champion elsewhere. These in turn come from town and county champs somewhere else. The list of national champion is not published annually. As of this writing the latest published list was in 2000, The lists are published in the magazine American Forests. You can also check the Internet for Register of Big Trees and you will find not only the National Register but also a number of regional registers.

If you decide to develop your own register of local and regional big trees, you may as well utilize the same measuring system as the National Register. This system combines several measurements on a point system to determine a rough estimate of the tree's volume. This helps eliminate arguments about one tree that is taller than another but smaller in circumference.

According to the American Forestry Association: "Trees are compared based on a total point score determined by adding the trunk circumference, measured in inches at 41/2 feet from the ground, plus the height of the tree in feet, plus one quarter of the average crown spread of the tree in feet."

If at some point you want to submit a nomination for the National Register of Big Trees, send the data to the American Forestry Association, 1319 Eighteenth St., N.W., Washington DC 20036. If you are interested in state registries, write the National Register and ask for the name and address of your state coordinator if one exists.

TREES AND GROWTH RINGS

During their growing seasons, trees lay down a record of seasonal weather condition at their site that permits the perceptive field botanist to build a historical record of changing condition there. During spring and early summer, tree stem cells grow rapidly and are larger; in winter growth is greatly reduced and cells are much smaller. In the cold of winter or the dry heat of summer, depending on the region's climate, no cells are produced. Thus, each yea produces an annular ring composed of one wide, light ring and one narrow, dark ring. In special cases, one year may have two such double bands; and in tropics, trees usually show no annual rings unless there is a wet/dry cycle climate.

Much can be deduced about a tree's historic struggle for existence by examining growth rings. If the tree has been cut, the rings can be examined and its life story read, at least approximately. A section with wide, even rings signifies a period of good conditions and fast growth. If these wide rings are followed by a section of increasingly narrow rings, it probably signifies increasing competition from neighbor trees. A widening of rings again is an indicator that somehow competition was reduced, perhaps because of blow-down of a neighboring tree or trees or a timber harvest. Of course, the narrow rings could also signify a drought period and the widening that follows a return to a heavier rainfall pattern. If the patter of narrow and wide rings is consistent for all the trees in the area, the regional weather pattern is probably the cause. If only a few scattered trees show the pattern, and then even in different years, competition is the more likely explanation. In some trees the pattern will not be very concentric; some sides of the tree will show wider growth rings on one side in a given year than on the other side. Here again competition is the big factor.

Obviously we don't want to cut down each tree to read its annular autobiography. There is another way to proceed, using an instrument called and **increment borer.** These are available in several sizes that remove different diameter cores up to about the size of a pencil. The instrument is horizontally twisted into a tree and extracts a core that shows a number of lines that are the seasonal rings. From these cores (which can be labeled, dried, and stored in plastic straws and capped at both ends for future reference), you can reconstruct the history of the tree.

Cores collected from woodlots throughout an area can be correlated to provide a fascinating history of the growth and success of the species in that woodland. Be aware that all the cores may represent trees of the same age, even though the trees seem markedly different in diameter. Tree core analysis may indicate approximately when that plot of land was last cleared for human use, burned over, or blown down. You will find many interesting things if you take a large sample of cores from a broad spectrum of species. Some species will show good growth followed by increasingly smaller rings. Other will show narrow rings at the center and then a period of wider and wider rings. Probably the first example came early in the succession but is being out competed by the second species, which had difficulty getting established but then began to get free of the competition of the first species and gained the upper hand. Increment borers are moderately expensive, but they do help enrich one's knowledge of a forest's recent past.

(Note: Removing a core provides an opening in the tee for potential infection by an insect or fungus pest. In caparison to the number of broken limbs and other naturally occurring gashes, the risk is not a great one—but it is a risk just the same. Plugging the hole where the core was removed with grafting wax will help reduce the risk)

OTHER WAYS TO DETERMINE GROWTH RATES

If you want to keep track of growth rates over the past three to five years—comparing growth among different branches, different individuals of the same species, or between different species—you may use terminal bud scale scars to determine each year's growth. Most woody plants in temperate regions have buds that develop into stems, leaves, and/or flowers. Most buds that opened this year were formed the previous season. Buds are found along the sides of stems located just above the axil where the leafstalk *(petiole)* joins the plant stem. As you may recall, these buds are called lateral or *axillary* buds. When a dead leaf falls off, it leaves a scar, so in winter we find axillary buds just above the leaf scars. In addition, terminal buds at the end of twigs characterize many species. Buds are usually enclosed in scales; when buds open, the bud scales fall and leave bud-scale scars. For terminal buds these bud—scale scars completely encircle the twig and remain visible on branchlets for several years until obliterated by increased growth of the bark.

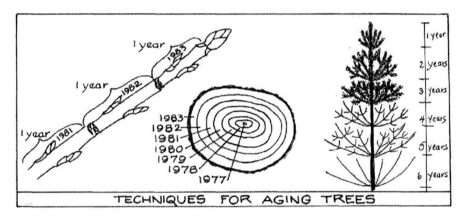

Figure 3-3

The distance between two sets of these encircling terminal bud-scale scars is one year's growth. (It is also the specific definition of a *twig.)* In autumn, winter, or early spring look back from the terminal bud to the first set of encircling bud-scale scars—that space represents growth during the previous summer. That summer's date is the year to be assigned to that section of the branch. If you are doing your study in the summer that same space represents the present year. Look back along branchlet and assign appropriate years until the scars are no longer visible.

Your may then want to correlate each years growth with a variety of environmental factors such as average rainfall during the appropriate year; number of days between the time frost left the ground in each particular year and ground re-freezing in autumn; percent of trees defoliated by insect pests such as gypsy moths; number of rainfalls with pH below some figure such as pH5;

or any of a number of other factors. Unfortunately, not all species have true terminal buds. A number have "false" terminal buds, for example, birches and poison ivy. Opposite these false terminal buds we find a short stub or scar that tells us where the seasons growth ended. False terminal buds are found directly over a leaf scar and are thus axillary rather than terminal buds. Species with false terminal buds can not be measured in the same way as those with true terminal buds

You can study annual growth in a number of pine species that have their buds in a whorl at the tips of their branches. Normally there is a central bud that will be the leader growing straight up, plus a surrounding crown of buds that will grow sideways. The distance between whorls of branches normally indicates one year's growth. Not infrequently the leader may be injured by insect, large browser, or mechanical injury of other kinds and will die.

When that occurs, one or more of the lateral branches usually reorients its position and assumes a somewhat vertical orientation as a new leader. Nonetheless, it still holds that the distance between whorls represents a year's growth. If you want to know approximately how high the pines were in the woodland twenty years ago, look to the top of the tree and count down twenty whorls. If you want to know how many years a go a pine woods was infested with white pine weevil, a pest that kills the leaders, count back the spaces from the top of the tree to a jog in the trunk where a side branch too over as leader. Some trees may have been victimized several times at different ages.

Professionals have fairly well determined the species of native trees growing in North America and, indeed, for many parts of the world, but much remains to be learned by amateurs and professionals alike about the life histories and ecological relationships of many species.

While trees have been well investigated, shrubs and vines, have received far less attention except for a comparatively few species. Shrubs tend to get their "day in the sun" in the middle of a number or successional sequences. In mature forest habitats, they generally end up as only minor members of the community understory.

Vines, or lianas, compete with trees and shrubs by clambering over them and using them for support. The leafy areas of many vines, such as kudzu and Japanese honeysuckle, may block out light from the very trees that support them, eventually killing those trees. Lianas are far more abundant in tropical and subtropical regions than in temperate ones. They use a number of strategies for reaching up to the top of the canopy. Some begin on the ground and climb up, while others have seeds that sprout high in the trees and grow down to the ground as well as up into the canopy. Parasitic vines, like dodder, begin as seeds in the ground. Their seedlings reach up and grasp a plant, penetrate its tissue with fingerlike processes called *haustoria,* and eventually break their contact with the ground altogether. They then spread over the autotrophic plant mass [1]with no further direct contact with the ground. Much remains to be learned about development of vines and lianas, their rates of growth, dispersal mechanisms, and many other aspects of their life histories and roles in plant communities.

AQUATIC FLOWERING PLANTS

Our wetlands and waterways are home to an extensive variety of flowering plants. Many grow only partly submerged; others are truly aquatic, living entirely submerged except at flowering time. It was once believed that such freshwater aquatic plants represented the transition of plants from saltwater dwellers to land dwellers, but today botanists feel sure that almost all freshwater flowering plants represent a return from the land to water. In a sense, freshwater environments represent a refugium for so me species that could not compete well on land.

Until recently, such aquatic groups were poorly studied. Emergent plants of shallow waters had received some attention, but submerged species were largely ignored. Perhaps the aquarium hobby did as much as anything to stimulate interest in submerged aquatic plants, triggering particular interest in species that might provide decoration for the aquaria. Many handsome species were discovered, along with a knowledge that they were not all easy to grow. Sensitive to water chemistry that supplies or mediates many nutrients and the vital gas exchange, many species prove very fussy to grow. Indeed, they often do best in the absence of the fish in which aquarists are primarily interested. Field studies of aquatic plants remain uncommon, getting far less attention than for terrestrial species.

Every type of wetland habitat has its unique aquatic species. A good initial project is to survey various wetlands of you area—bog, marshes, swamps, ponds, lakes, streams, and rivers—to determine what species live in which habitat. Some will show up in more than one habitat; others will be restricted to only one. Gather data on the amount of time each year that the overall site is underwater and how the depth of the water varies through the seasons. If these data are mapped, they often reveal a number of depth zones and/or zones of inundation. If you map the dominant species, chances are you will find a strong correlation between the plant species and these zones. Not all wetlands are fresh-water; in coastal areas the water may be brackish or salt, subject to tidal flooding.

After some exploration, you will probably note that certain species can tolerate having their roots and lower stems underwater for a period of weeks or months as long ass their leaves are above water. Others have adapted to total submersion for most of their life history, poking up into the air primarily to carry on their reproductive rites. These two major groupings need to be explored with slightly different techniques. Emergent species can be studied with most of the same approaches you employ with land plants, except that you must also gather information on water depth and water chemistry. In most cases, emergent vegetation grows in water less than waist deep. Of importance is the nature of the substrate. It may be gravelly, clayey, sandy, or rather thick organic ooze. The first types are easy to work in; but clay and ooze can be a problem, often being deep and exerting sucking forces almost like quicksand. Ooze must be treated with caution and respect.

Transects across wetlands from dry land out to chest-deep water reveal many subtleties about the preferences or tolerances of various species, and relatively small changes may have strong influences on which species are present or absent. In addition to the actual water level at the time of you investigation, try to find out information on normal high and low water levels for that body of water.

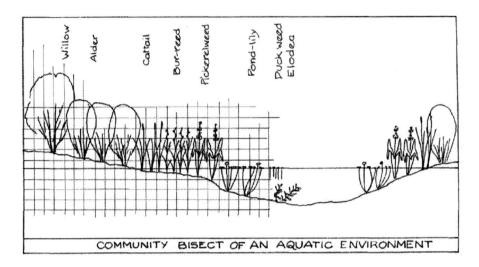

Figure 3-4

It is relatively easy to record the location of each along your transect, if plants are growing as isolated individuals, If the plants are reproducing vegetatively, forming dense patches of a single species, record the distance along the transect where a patch begins and ends (i.e. eelgrass patch—5m to 8m). Represent the data on a scaled version of the transect with symbols to represent each species. See Figure 3-4

Seeing beneath the water surface in shallow water is often difficult because of reflections. It is very helpful to build and use a simple water—scope (essentially a clear plastic or glass-bottomed bucket). Placing the bottom of the bucket below water and viewing through it will give you a much clearer perception of what is happening at the base of the plants, and the nature of the substrate. Waters-copes are a bit awkward to handle until you get the knack, but they are worth the effort for what they permit you to observe. When you work beyond waist-depth, a snorkel and mask can replace the water-scope.

There are extensive questions yet to be answered about the autecology of many aquatic species and about their phenology. When do the plants emerge from the dormant period and when do they go dormant? When do they begin flowering? Under what condition do they flower rather than reproduce vegetatively? For instance, duckweeds (*Lemna*) are on of our tiniest flowering plants, but they flower rarely; under what conditions do they do this? What animals have effects on the various aquatic species? Does a species have clear-cut tolerances for certain substrates, chemical conditions of the water, or strength of current in flowing waters?

Habitat Study of Aquatic Plants

Because submerged plants are in such intimate contact with their environment, the observer of aquatic plants has only a limited view of what is going on if he or shed does not gather information on physical and chemical characteristic of the body of water in which they are growing. Basic testing can be don with one of the various testing kits available from **Hach Chemical Company**(Box 907, Ames, IA 50010) and **LaMotte Chemical** company (Chestertown, MD 21620. Gather information on dissolved oxygen and carbon dioxide, for these gases play a major role in a plant's ability to respire and photosynthesize, respectively. Also test for soluble salts in the water which can serve as nutrients for the plants, or which may be pollutants. Data on pH and alkalinity are likewise important; the latter indicates something of that water's ability to buffer acidity. To get useful readings take water samples from various depths because the chemical factors often show vertical gradation.

Among the physical factors to be explored is turbidity, or color of the water since this affects the depth to which light can penetrate and thus the light quality and intensity available to submerged plants. This information can be gathered from a boat by lowering a black-and-white patterned Secchi disc and noting the depth at which it disappears from view. Reading may vary throughout the season because of changing turbidity from heavy rains that increase silt in the water or from blooms of plankton.

When exploring stream and river plants, be sure to gather information on the length of the stream section explored and, at various points, collect measurements of the breadth and depth of the stream and the rate of flow (velocity) of the water. You can do the latter by timing a floating stick or cork's movement between a measured distance. If you do not have equipment with you to measure stream velocity can extrapolate a rough estimate by noting the size of the material on the streambed. The British ecologist S.G. Tansely determined the following relationships:

SUBSTRATE	VELOCITY IN FT/SEC.	VELOCITY IN M/SEC
Rock	4+	1.2+
Heavy shingle	3-4	0.91-1.21
Light shingle	2-3	0.60-0.91
Gravel	1-2	0.30-0.60
Sand	8"-1	0.20-0.30
Silt	5"-8"	0.12-0.20
Mud	0-5	-0.12>

MARINE SEAWEEDS

Some people are attracted to the sea as if by a magnet, and those with a botanical bent can find a whole new world to explore there. Although a few species of flowering plants live in the shallow waters, Kingdom Plantae is essentially replaced in marine environments by various phyla of the Kingdom Protoctista. This is the realm of the red, green, and brown algae and their relatives.

For landlubbers there must be a whole new orientation because the vegetation here is not one they have grown up with and the "plants" all seem unusually strange and confusing. Their life cycles are complex, often alternating between microscopic forms and relatively large forms—indeed, some of the giant kelps rival redwood trees for title of world's tallest plants. However, after spending time with a few appropriate field guides to acquire a mental picture of some of the more common species to be encountered, people are ready to enter the marine realm and familiarize themselves with these plants on their home ground. It does not take long to realize that in the ocean, as on land, the various species tend to grow in association with others, forming communities. They encounter grazers, parasites, and diseases as do land plants. Different substrates host different species, and there are vertical zones with distinctive association as well as horizontal expanses of just a few species. Following plant activity in an area throughout a year or more reveals that, as on land, some species are perennial and others annual. In short, both major realms show similar broad patters of living while varying widely in detail.

Many of the same techniques used for observing plants on land can be adapted to life beneath the waves and between the tides. Transect lines can be run from above the tide line out to any depth to which you are skilled enough to dive. Quadrats can be established. Underwater trails can be laid out that can become routine routes for your observation of an area. Observations are to be made on the appearance and disappearance of annual species and these correlated to environmental changes. Successional patterns of plant communities can be determined. Animal associates and their impact on the plants should be noted.

But there are some major differences that must be taken into account. Marine botanists must learn to differentiate between organisms that are autotrophic members of the Protoctista or Plantae and the hetero-trophic Animalia that are sessile and loosely resemble plants in form. There are also different hazards to be encountered and dealt with, such as slippery rocks in the tidal zone; the tides themselves; tidal currents; and local organisms that may sting, bite, or perforate.

Marine botanists need essentially the same aquatic skills outlined in the section on freshwater plants. In general, marine habitats are more diverse than fresh water ones, and the forces of tidal surge and currents provide greater hazards. If you intend to undertake marine plant exploration, be sure your SCUBA skills ore well developed and carefully follow all safety procedures. This is particularly important when studying rocky coasts. Much can be learned about the zonation when the tide is out, but to get food understanding of a community at work, it has to be observed underwater. It is all too easy for tidal surge or wave action to thrust the unwary diver hard against a rock. Also, as you, an inquisitive marine botanist, move into deeper water and into kelp forests, caution must be taken not to get yourself or you equipment tangled in the long fronds.

LICHENS

Figure 3-5

Most people think of lichens as some kind of plant but they are a strange combination of two very different organisms living together in a partnership. One of these organisms is a heterotropic fungus and an autotrophic alga. Ever since the discovery of this partnership of these two different life forms, it has bee widely proclaimed as a classic example of symbiosis. Originally people conceived of symbiosis as two organisms living together for mutual benefit. Today such a relationship is called *mutualism* Mutualism is thought of as only one aspect of living together along with such other aspects such a *parasitism*—where one partner benefits at the expense of another—and *commensalism*—where one partner profits but there is neither significant benefit or expense to the other. Results of recent research still point to the lichen relationship as a symbiotic one but present it as a range of degrees of parasitism rather that mutualism. Lichenologist Mason Hale has called it "balanced parasitism", The fungal partner, which gives structural form to a lichen, is absolutely dependent on the algal partner and. most species, cannot survive without it. On the other hand, the algal species can, and do, live without the fungus and may even grow better without it. In a number of cases, more than one algal species may be the partner of a specific lichen fungus. Our understanding of lichens is growing and changing. Although most lichen study goes on in the laboratory and involves meticulous technical procedure there are lichen investigation s to be undertaken by the field botanist.

TRACKING LICHEN GROWTH RATES

One area of exploration is lichen growth rates. Lichens grow exceedingly slowly, probably because they contain significantly less chlorophyll than regular green plants. It has been suggested that, at least for some species, individual growth may follow a logarithmic progression rather than an arithmetic one, growth being faster as the plant matures. More extended field studies with have to be carried out to confirm or deny this. Photograph lichens, taking care to put paint or other markers on the surface where the plant is growing so you can return to the spot again and again to re-photograph exactly the same area. Mounting a millimeter ruler at on edge of he focal area where the divisions on it can be clearly seen clarifies the magnification. A problem with such a photographic method is the need to use a small f-stop such an f-16 or-f-22 to get maximum depth of field while working close up. Also measure and record the exact distance from the center of the spot to be pictured. Since many lichens prefer sunny, exposed locations, this may not be too difficult, but be prepared to use flash when necessary.

A different method involves placing a transparent plastic sheet over the place where the lichens are growing and then tracing the outline of the outline using the colored markers designed for preparing overhead transparencies. Mark the locations of the corners of your transparent sheet on the tree or rock substrate with paint (model airplane dope works well) do you can replace the plastic sheet exactly at a later date and retrace the outline of the plants, preferably with a different color each time, These overlays will show not only the amount of growth but the degree of evenness around the plant.

Do your tracings or photographs at regular intervals, perhaps every three months or once a year to begin with. Be sure to give each tracing station a code number and put it on the transparency, or on a card that will show in your photo. This will help you to match the right tracing or photo to the proper station. L Use the photos or tracings to calculate the rate of growth on a graph and determine whether it produce a logarithmic cur or an arithmetic straight line.

There area three basic lichen growth forms. Very tiny plants that look like a scaly crust and grow primarily on rock characterize one form. These *crustose* lichens are very hardy; some even live in the spaces between rock crystals of snow-free Antarctic rocks! Crustos lichens are very difficult for an amateur to identify, and there are no identification keys for amateurs for these species. The second form has leaf-like thalli, often in rosette patterns. These are the *foliose* (from the Latin for "leaf") lichens. The third growth form takes the shape of upright structures of diverse shapes such as goblet, minarets, and open sponges. These are the *fruiticose* lichens. Fruticose species need to be recorded three dimensionally; photographs work best.

Take careful note of where the various lichen species are found and the substrates upon which they reside. This involves gaining familiarity with rock types as well as recognizing trees by their bark. Different types of rock are acidic or basic and the lichen species have preferences. Lichens get their minerals primarily from rainwater and dew. Which mineral they get is dependent upon what the water has passed over and dissolved. Some lichens also show preferences for certain species of trees and particular exposure and heights above ground. These data should be noted so you can determine whether a species has a preferential or undifferentiated distribution pattern in the community.

Theoretically, cities provide many good places for lichens to thrive but instead of increasing with urban expansion, lichens are on the decline there. This is because of their sensitivity to air pollutants, particularly sulfur dioxide .($SO2$). Urban plant observers can scout metropolitan areas to map the locations of the different species of lichens. The resulting maps often reveal much about the intensity and drift patterns of air pollution in the region. By repeating the search and mapping every few years, it is possible to determine increases or reduction in local air pollution.

Much remains to be discovered about ways in which lichens disperse and colonize in the wild. Although the fungal elements of the partnership form spores, an you can usually find spore-bearing structures on the lichen thallus, no one has yet observed a developing fungal spore recruiting or capturing algae to form a functioning lichen plant. All observed lichen reproduction appears to be vegetative.

Three major lichen structures, in addition to pieces of broken primary thallus, permit vegetative reproduction: *isidia*, *soredia* (or *soralia*), and *squamules*. Insidia are very tiny, coral—like outgrowths of the upper layer of the lichen thallus. About fifteen percent of foliose lichen species possess them. And isidia are often used as clues to species identification in lichen keys. Soredia are interior structures that lead to the surface where they erupt in powdery clumps called soralia. Soralia are found in six different patterns, depending upon the species. About thirty percent of lichens have them. Their powdery texture differentiates them from isidia. The powder consists of clumps of algal cells enmeshed in some fungal hyphae. Certain lichens, like those of the common genus *Cladonia*. Have a base composed of many scale-like thalluses called squamules that can break off to form new individuals. This is particularly common among soil lichens that get trampled by animals.

Much remains to be observed concerning how these structures get freed from the parent plant and are transported. Look carefully at appropriate substrates with your hand lens to see if you can locate any pieces isidia, dust from soredia, or tiny squamules. When you do mark them and watch and record their progress. Remember that patience is a virtue, so. too, is persistence.

You will, of course, want to identify the lichen species you are investigating. Fortunately, A number of kinds are quite easy to identify to the species level, while others can readily be assigned to the genus. Unfortunately, a larger number can accurately be identified only through a series of chemical tests. A serious amateur can learn to do these tests and the latest lichen keys explain how. However, most people prefer to send a specimen to a lichen expert a state university or a museum for identification.

At present there are no organizations devoted solely to lichens, but many papers on lichens are published in *The Bryologist* and many lichen enthusiasts belong to the American Bryological and Lichenology Society. Even though lichens are more closely related to fungi, many people still tend to think of them as somehow allied with mosses and liverworts with which they frequently grow.

4

LIVING WITHIN
THE PHYSICAL
ENVIRONMENT

Amateur and professional field botanists need to investigate the physical environment in which a plan is growing, for it it is that with which the plant is in most intimate and extensive contact. From it a plant must extract all of the raw materials and nutrients needed for photosynthesis and growth. The quality and nature of the intimate environment will stimulate physical adaptation of the plant or determine its failure to survive. It is not possible to understand the world of a plant unless you understand the kinds of environment it can tolerate and those kinds, which it prefers and in which it thrives vigorously.

In large measure animals depend on electrical impulses to transmit messages about their interactions with environment throughout the organism, but they also have a significant number of chemical messengers. With plants the weighting is reversed. Chemical messengers with only a tiny fraction by electrical impulse, in a few species, carry out the majority of internal and external communications. Plants also have broad contact with the air, water, and soil about them and respond intimately chemicals they encounter there. In a real sense, plants are nature's master chemists. Humans have been profiting from their chemistry from earliest times, finding in plants chemicals for healing and making products like rubber, fibers, and dyes. Of course, plants also make chemicals toxic to other life forms, thus providing the plant a modicum of protection from predators (remember, to a plant herbivores are predators) or a barrier to invasion of their space by other plants. We see the latter particularly among goldenrods and some desert plants such as sagebrush.

To understand fully the many complex interaction between plants and their environment, we would have to delve into the complex arena of plant physiology, which is essentially a laboratory science that involves a long academic background and sophisticated techniques and equipment. That fascinating subject is well beyond the scope of this book. However, clues to problems to be investigated by the plant physiologist often come from the observations of field botanists. A field botanist observes what, when, where, and under what conditions a plant lives and dies; a plant physiologist tries to determine how and perhaps why.

GETTING ACQUAINTED WITH SOILS

Not all plants require soil, although most plants require some substrate to which they attach for all or part of their life cycle. For some the substrate is wood, peat, or tree bark, but for the majority it is soil.

For many people soil is just so much dirt. Such a view derives from lack of familiarity with this precious commodity that represents the interface of the three great physical spheres of our planet—the lithosphere, (the planetary rock), the atmosphere (the gaseous envelope) and the hydrosphere (the areas of liquid and frozen water). Soils are made up of five basic components: rock particles, air, water, living organisms, and organic materials. The latter are the products of living organisms (feces, cast skins, dead leaves, and the decaying remains of plants and animals).

As you might imagine, the variation in size and composition of rock particles and organic material and the changing percentages of air and water, create an immense number of possible mixes that generate quite different soils. The fundamental nature of local soils is a result of the geologic history and current topography of the land. Some soil types remain fairly constant for long periods of time, while others undergo relatively rapid change. Development of soils over times results in identifiable *soil types* somewhat akin to plant and animal species. These different types are recognizable and have been named and mapped. In the United States you can check with your local conservation district and/or the USDA Soil Conservation Service District Office that services it, to find out if the area you are studying has been mapped according to soil types. If it has, you may want to acquire such a map. The Soil Conservation Service also has booklets describing the characteristics of each soil type and listing some of their capabilities for plant growth, at least for agriculturally important plants.

There is much you can learn on your own about the local soils and their characteristics even if you don't have a soils map. Indeed, the scale of many maps is such that one soil type is shown over and area that actually includes a number of small pockets of other soil types too small to map accurately. Because plants may actually be confined to those pockets, it is prudent to do some soil data gathering during your field observations even if you do have the local soils map.

SOIL CHARACTERISTIC S

Particle size. An important way of classifying soils is by the various particle sizes and the percent of each in a standard sample. At each site gather a level measuring cup full of soil and pour it into a pint jar. Fill the jar with water, shake thoroughly, then set the jar aside and let the particles settle. As the soil settles, if will form stratified layers. The largest particles will be on the bottom and the smallest on top with some bits of clay so small that they remain suspended in the water for many hours or even days. Organic material may float at the surface. Be sure to label each sample and key it to the plant observations in your field journal.

Figure 4-1

Soil scientists have a specific size-range definition for each of the component particles:

Fine gravel (2mm-lmm)   Very fine sand (0.10mm-0.o5mm)

Coarse sand (lmm-0.5mm)   Silt (0.05mm-0.002m)

Medium sand (0.5mm-0.25mm)   Clay (below 0.002mm)

Fine sand (0.35-0.10mm)

Using the technique of a shaken bottle of soil, it is not easy to differentiate the silt and clay; however after a few hours silt will usually settle out while clay remains suspended.

If you consistently use the same kind of pint jar, you can collect data by taping a strip of paper to the side of the jar before shaking it. Once the settling-out has occurred, carefully mark onto the paper strip the dividing point between each layer. After each layer is labeled, the strip can be removed from the jar and mounted in your journal.

By looking at the rough percentages of different soil particle sizes you will be able to classify the soils into three fundamental groups and a variety of subtypes as indicated in the following chart:

Sandy soil	Loamy sails	Clay soils
gravelly sands	medium sandy loams	stony clays
coarse sands	stony sandy loams	gravelly clays
medium sands	coarse sandy loams	sandy clays
fine sands	coarse sandy loams	silty clays
very fine sands	very fine sandy loams	clays
	loams, gravelly loams	
and stony loams		
	silty loams and stony	
	siltloams	
	silty clay loams	
	clay loams	
	stony clay loams	

Notice that the name of the particle size with the highest percentage provides the last word of this soil type while the firs and/or second word modifiers indicate particle sizes mixed in lesser amounts. A brief description of the major soil groups may help you understand plants' environments.

Sands. A sandy soil has less than twenty percent by weight of silt and clay, it is quite porous, and thus has fast drainage. Sand particles are not very cohesive and their soils crumble very easily.

Clays. Soils with thirty percent or more clay particles are classified as clays. These soils may have even more silt than clay, but as long as the requisite amount of clay is present they are still classified as clays. Clay particles, along with being very small, usually carry an electrical charge that helps bind the together making clay soils extremely sticky and slippery to the touch. The minute particle size and general compactness means that little air or water can circulate in these soils.

Loams. It is more difficult to define loams than sands and clays, because loam is really a mixture of sand, silt and clay. This mixture normally results in a soil whose particles cling together well yet also has good porosity for air and water circulation, making loams a food growing medium for a wide variety of plants. There is also usually a fair amount or organic material. As you would expect, the percentage of the various components in the mix changes the character of the loam and its suitability for any particular plant species.

Gravels. We did not mention gravel as a major soil type, but there are places where the soil is largely composed of gravel, such as in some deserts, piedmont plains, alluvial fans, river bars and delta, glacial deposits, scree slopes on mountains, and many built environments. There are some specialized plants that do survive, even thrive, in such soils and that may be found almost exclusively in such places.

SOIL COMPOSITION AND TEXTURE

A soil is more than just the rock particles in it—it is the total mix with air, water, organisms, and organic material. The various particles bring more than size to the mixture, and their individual properties often change the characteristics of the resulting mix. Because clay particles are quite plastic, when moisture is present the can press together and adhere. If the same particles dry, they shrink together, crack, and store potential energy. When they re-wet, the may give off that potential energy as heat. Clays also absorb water, gases, and soluble salts at a high rate, which makes them valuable in a soil mix for supplying nutrients to plants. Silt has many of the same properties as clay but to a lesser degree. Soils with a high percentage of silts and clays become sticky when wet and form hard clods when dry, resulting in expansion and contraction of these soils. Yet in smaller quantities, they are an important reason for loams being a good growth medium for many species.

Decayed organic matter is an important part of a soil for many plant species since it is a source of nutrients. It is not surprising that since sands and clays support less life than do loams, they generally have smaller amounts of organic matter. Living plants and their decaying litter affect soil in other ways as well. Water dripping down the plants and percolating through the litter leaches humic acids and other chemicals downward and/or outward. Through complex reaction, these chemicals cause soil particles to form clumps, often referred to as crumbs or aggregates. These vary in size and, because the spaces (pores) between them, increase the capacity of the soil to hold water and circulate air they affect the structure of the soil. Soil structure has a definite impact on root development and vigor.

You can get some sense of the texture of solid in places where you are observing plants by passing a soil sample through a series of sieves of decreasing mesh size. Examine the coarser particles carefully. Are they solid, or will they crush between your fingers and pass through the mesh? If they do, they are aggregates. What percentage of material at each mesh size is aggregate material? Given the same mix of basic materials, some plants will survive only in a soil of good structure—that is, a good percentage of various size aggregates. This particularly true of soils that tend to be somewhat clayey.

Another factor that affects soil structure is *compaction*, which can be generated from the weight of temporary standing water such as from flooding or from the regular passage of animals or vehicles. Compaction usually occurs in relatively small areas or zones, such as along trail or roadway, and it can modify a soil's normal capacity to support particular species of plants. In some exposed soils, the force of falling raindrops may compact the surface of the soil, preventing insoak of the rain and fostering puddling or runoff of the water. If you see plants distributed in such a way that there are zones where a species is either excluded or where it exists exclusively, check for soil compaction.

The simplest way to check soil compaction is to take a pencil, place the point in the ground, and put the eraser end against the center of your palm. Press down until it hurts your palm to push farther. Measure how far the pencil penetrates the soil. Repeat at various sites, stopping at the same level of discomfort each time. Compare the amounts of penetration

Both texture and structure of soil affect its ability to hold moisture and circulate air; I soil some percentage of pore spaces between particles occupied by either air or water is in constant flux. Roots of some species can endure saturated soils while others cannot. It is difficult to get accurate readings of the changing soil moisture in the field, but you can take regular readings with one of the electronic moisture indicators now available for use with houseplants or you can use the following water absorption method.

For the latter, cut both ends out of a large juice can. Push the can and inch or so into the soil and then pour in a quart of water. Rime how long it takes for the full quart to be absorbed below the surface. The method is crude but provides a rough indication of the water-holding capacity of the soil at that point in time and space.

Some plant species are more efficient than others at tapping water that clings as a thin film to the surface of rock particles. These species may continue to do well in a soil that appears quite dry. There is also dew that condenses on the soil surface at night, sometimes even during dry spells, and which is utilized by some shallow rooted species.

SOIL DEVELOPMENT

Soils are dynamic and constantly changing, albeit slowly. They evolve from the weathering of bedrock or deposits of materials eroded by wind, water, or glacial ice. In the dry southwest, many of the soils lie almost directly above the parent rocks, particularly in the flat regions. Soils of the continent's glaciated regions range from fairly thin toppings to deep deposits of glacial till. Slope affects the three dimensional nature of soils, with materials eroding from steep areas and depositing on flatter ones.

A soil must therefore be considered in three dimensions. In addition to its surface area, it has a depth and a layered structure. This results in a characteristic *soil profile* when a cutaway is dug. Each mature soil type has a characteristic profile that indicates something about the concentration of minerals and the availability of water. Such characteristics affect the activity and location of underground plant parts.

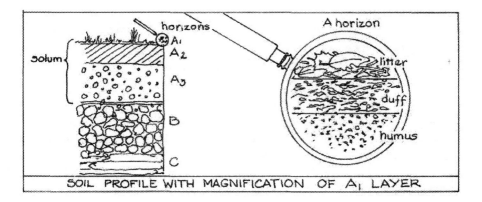

Figure 4-2

In large measure, the nature of the different layers is caused by the degree of weathering. Soils forming under similar conditions of parent material, topography, rainfall, and biological influence will show similar profiles and probably grow plants of similar requirements. Those soils that are of similar nature and sequences of layers, or horizons, can be named and classified in much the same way as plants and animals.

A soil profile usually has three major horizons, These are conventionally designated from the top down as the *A-horizon, B-horizon, and C-horizon.* If the soil structure warrants it, individual horizons may be subdivide into component layers denoted by a subscript to the major horizon, such as A_1, A_2, and so on.

The A-horizon generally contains the most organic material, and this may be classified by the degree of decay. The top layer, or *litter*, contains plant or animal parts that are virtually intact and recognizable. Beneath this is a layer of material call *duff* that is composed of pieces of litter in only barely recognizable form. Below this is *humus*, a more fully decayed material, generally dark in color, mixed in with the soil. The A-horizon is in contact with rain, and in humid regions chemicals in this layer may be rapidly leached downward to accumulate in the B-horizon. The two horizons are generally recognizable by differences in color. Depending upon the soil type, the leached materials can be such things as iron, aluminum, clay, or calcium carbonate, and other salts. Together the A-and B—horizons are developed through the soil-building process and are collectively known as he *solum*. Most subterranean plant activity occurs in the solum.

The C-horizon is the less weathered material lying between the solum and the bedrock. As time passes and upper layers of the C-horizon weather further, they too will become part of the solum.

You can collect data on the soil profile near plants you are exploring using a soil auger. This device, which resembles an oversize drill bit, allows you to twist up samples of soil to measure the depth and color changes of the various horizons. You may wish to take soil samples from different depths and test them for minerals, pH, and other factors. You may find that conditions at depths where the bulk of the plant's root activity takes place are quite different from those at the surface. Soil samplers that remove a solid care of soil are also available commercially.

The rate at which solid develop is quite variable, but in all cases it is slow by human reckoning. At its fastest, natural soil development usually takes a century or more. Soil development is generally most rapid in cool, humid climates, but rapid development is compromised by poorer quality because the moisture in such climates leaches the A-horizon of its nutrients. Under natural condition, percolation through fallen leaves makes the soil water acid. This is accentuated by the phenomenon of acid deposition, often popularly called "acid rain". Acid water dissolves out the majority of any calcium carbonate present and deposit aluminum and iron compounds in the B-horizon. This leaching/deposition process id called *podzolization*, and the resulting soils are classified as *podzols*. True podzoles have an ashy-gray horizon and the term is derived from the Russian *pod*, meaning "under" and *zola*, meaning "ash".

Soils develop very slowly in cool but sub-humid climates, and the resulting prairie soils, or *chernozems*, are superior in quality to podzols, at least for many important crops. Chernozems (the Russian word for black soil) concentrate calcium carbonate in the B-horizon, and therefore these soils are distinctly less acid than podzols. This deposition process is known as calcification. In sub-tropical and tropical regions, other soil development processes, *latasolation* and *laterization*, are at work. Soil derived from both processes lack distinct horizons; both decompose and dissipate silicon dioxide from the topsoil and form deposits of iron oxide that give these deep soils a red or yellow color. In areas of heavy rainfall these soils are usually severely leached of plant nutrients. In humid tropical areas, plants must get more of their nutrients from above the ground than below. Most nutrients are incorporated in the growing plants. Cleared of vegetation for any appreciable time, laterites bake rock-hard and exclude new vegetation.

SOIL NUTRIENTS

As a plant observer, you may not want to get deeply involved in chemical analysis of soil, but it is useful to become familiar with basic soil-testing procedures and to keep data on the levels of key nutrients in the habitats of species you are studying. Such information may reveal clues about the apparent state of health and vigor of plants you are observing and may come in handy when you are trying to create optimum condition for relocating wild plants to a study garden or conservation area.

pH

A simple test to begin with is one for pH. This will measure how basic (alkaline) or acidic the soil is. Testing is accomplished by measuring free hydrogen ions either with an indicator paper that changes color in the presence of specific concentration of the ions, or with an electronic pH meter available from some garden supply stores.

Various nutrients and their components exist as soluble salts dissolved in soil water. In solution, the compounds disassociate and chemical *ions* (electrically charged particles are released. Hydrogen (H) ions have a positive electrical charge; hydroxyl (OH) ions have a negative electrical charge. In a soil solution composed of more H ions than OH ions, the condition is described as being acidic. When the reverse is true, the soil is said to be alkaline. When a balance exists between these two ions, the situation is neutral.

Recorded on a logarithmic scale, pH is defined as the logarithm of the reciprocal of the H ion concentration. It is not essential that you understand its derivation, but you should understand that each unit of change of the scale reflects a tenfold increase or decrease in the degree of acidity or alkalinity; the pH8 is ten times more alkaline than pH7. Plant species vary greatly in their preferences and tolerances of pH. The chart below indicates some pH values and their interpretation

pH above 8.0   very alkaline

pH 7.4-8.0   alkaline

pH 6.6-7a.3   neutral or nearly so (7.0 is true neutral)

pH 6.0-6.5   slightly acid

pH 5.5-5.9   moderately acid

pH 5.0-5.4   strongly acid

pH 4.3-4.9   very strongly acid

pH below 4.3   extremely acid

While pH is not a direct measurement of any soil nutrients, it does reflect the chemistry of the soil and thus the availability of soil nutrients. In general, the more acid the soil, the greater has been the leaching of the nutrients.

NITROGEN, PHOSPHORUS AND POTASSIUM

Nitrogen is an important nutrient for most plants. Nitrogen depletion can result in stunted top growth and poor root growth. On the other hand, too much nitrogen will cause retardation of maturation and decreased disease resistance in some species. Nitrogen favors development of leaves.

Phosphorus affects many basic plant functions. Cell division can't take place without it, and it facilitates the conversion of starch to sugars. Seeds do not form without it, and flowering and fruiting depend upon it. Phosphorus will has will hasten maturation and thus may counter the effects of nitrogen excess.

Potassium affects the general tone and vigor of any plant. It increases resistance to certain diseases and stimulates development of the root system. Essential for the formation of starch and the movement of sugars, potassium also facilitates utilization of carbon dioxide, nitrogen and the uptake of water. When it is too concentrated, it delays maturation.

You may have noticed that the different nutrients often have contradicting effects on the plant Thus we are interested not only in the presence of these nutrients but in their relative abundance, because suitability of a soil for a particular species depends upon the relative amounts and interplay of these substances and often of other that are more difficult to measure.

The above basic nutrients can be practically measured in a soil by meticulously following the directions in a good soil test kit. Sudbury, Hach, and LaMotte are all reliable manufacturers of such kits. If you are not performing the tests in the field be sure to label each sample carefully and keep the samples in clean container that seal tightly to reduce risk of accidental contamination. Label the samples location and preferably use a map to refer the samples to.

Unfortunately, extensive soil testing can get to be expensive as you purchase replacement chemical for the kits. On the other than, relatively little is known about specific nutrient level preferences of most wild plants, so any measurements you systematically make may turn out to be significant.

In taking nutrient levels to determine a species preferences, be sure to take readings where the species is not growing as well as where it is to see if differences exist. If, after mapping the distribution individuals or population of a species, you suspect some clear patterns of occurrence, run transect lines through the pattern and into areas outside the distribution zone. Check nutrient levels and other abiotic factors like temperature, moisture, light intensity, and soil type at a number of points along the transect lines. Map the data for each factor and connect points with the same value. Compare the maps. Does the data create patterns that are similar to the plant distribution map? It may take some statistical analysis, sometimes of a very sophisticated nature, to confirm correlation of a particular degree of a factor with a plant's distribution;

however, the simple mapping comparisons often provide a first step towards more detailed research.

The physical environment provides for far more of a plant's needs than just nutrients and other chemicals. Water and energy are other major requirements. The degree to which these environmental factors can be explored by the average amateur depends upon access to, or lack of access to, expensive and sophisticated measuring tools. Nonetheless, a plant observer should pay attention to these environmental factors in a plant's life and record as much data as is practical concerning them.

ENERGY

Two major aspects of environmental energy, heat and light can be measured relatively easily and with comparatively inexpensive equipment.

In green plants the amount of heat available in air and soil affects a host of plant activities from seed germination to rate of cell division and thus growth. Each plant species tends to have a range of heat tolerance with four critical points and a middle range representing optimal growth. The four critical points are: low temperature, where death occurs; low temperature, where growth stops and dormancy begins; high temperature where growth stops and dormancy begins; and high temperature that kills. Each species also has a critical time period when the temperature must remain within the optimum range; this is the growing season. If weather conditions are unusual and the growing season is significantly shortened in any year, plants may not be able to produce seed. Thus, in some cases, whole populations may be killed outright, altering the distribution patter of the species in the area.

Because of variation in topography, temperature conditions are seldom constant over extensive areas. Usually there are thousands of mini-climates and microclimates where temperatures are higher or lower than the average for the surrounding environment, resulting in a checkerboard pattern of survival and loss among populations of species in any particular region. Warm-blooded animals that maintain fairly constant body temperatures are less affected by temperature fluctuations than their "cold-blooded" relatives. Plants are much more like those cold-blooded animals, their body temperature are seldom much cooler or warmer than the surrounding environment. A few notable exceptions have been uncovered. Common skunk cabbages push up through freezing soil of the marsh by generating enough heat to exceed that of their surroundings. Thus, the soil immediately around them is thawed. Also, the internal temperature of pine needles in winter has been found to be warmer than he surrounding air by as much as 10 degrees or more.

When there is a sudden change in environmental temperature, for a while there will be a marked difference between it and the plant's internal temperature. This is primarily because of the water in the plant that takes longer to heat and cool than air does. This delay factor allows most plants to withstand a brief exposure to lethal temperatures. Thus, man species endure the first isolated frost of autumn or survive a midday spell or withering heat. Since the sun delivers its most direct rays at midday, it might seem reasonable to expect highest temperatures then, but there is always a time lag as the various materials of air and earth take on solar energy and heat up. Consequently, you can look for highest temperatures around 2:30 p.m, and the coolest just a little before sunrise. These are the times when temperatures are best recorded if you anticipate them to be in the critical ranges. Ecologists use thermographs to provide a continuous recording of temperature, but these are generally too expensive for the average observer. Maximum/minimum thermometers are a little more affordable but are still quite expensive if you need several to explore a number of plant locations at the same time. Simple thermometers or thermistors are more practical but they require more effort on the observer's part.

Unfortunately, general temperature information available from radio, television, or from your home thermometer is of little value in plant observations. Topographical variation affects how the sun's rays strike a particular place and for how long. Likewise, the color of soil and vegetation influences how much energy is absorbed and how much is reflected away. These variations, in turn, affect the air and soil temperature. Temperature varies considerably at different distances from the ground surface. All this adds up to considerable differences among local microclimates, those little pockets of climate located in particular places. Two species growing only a few feet from one another may dwell in remarkable different microclimates. Thus, the plant observer is well advised to make many and regular temperature readings over several seasons to determine what may be the temperature optimums and limiting extremes for a species.

Where and when possible, you will want to note soil temperatures as well as air temperatures taken primarily at the height of most leaves. Because temperature affects growth rate, and air warms faster than soil, stem and leaf growth may start earlier than root growth. Likewise, because soil temperature remains warmer longer, in temperate climates root growth may continue after stem and leaf activity have greatly slowed down or ceased. Among perennials this can be important because the roots give major physical and nutrient support to the next growing season's stem and leaf growth.

Physical topography is not the only factor that affects temperature regimes; vegetation type influences microclimates considerably. Taller, broad-leaved vegetation blocks sunlight from falling directly on the soil, thus slowing down temperature buildup there. It also helps cool air near the ground. Depending upon a species' requirements, these ground and soil temperatures will help determine which seed can sprout and whether resulting seedlings can put on enough growth to become established. Temperature can have a powerful effect on which species survive and which do not at any given station. It has a potent effect on the flora of a region though not necessarily on the vegetation. That, the types of plants that can survive in an area may be grasses or broad-leaved deciduous plants, and temperature won't change that; what it is likely to affect is which species of grasses or broad-leaved plants will survive and dominate.

In hilly country, it is important to check which direction the slopes are facing and their altitude. These factors can have a strong impact on temperature and thus on the composition of species that will thrive there. Species growing on a north-facing slope may differ markedly from those growing on a south-facing slope just across the valley or ravine. Such differences of exposure may create isolated pockets (*refugia*) for species Normally found in more northerly or southerly regions. Increasing altitude with less dense air results in more rapid heat loss and thus cooler average condition than those of lower altitude. Average conditions at higher altitudes are usually derived from greater daily extremes and plants have to have tolerance for such. The microclimate factors strongly affect the distribution of plant species, creating vertical bands of plant communities as altitude increases. Each higher band corresponds to communities of more northern latitudes.

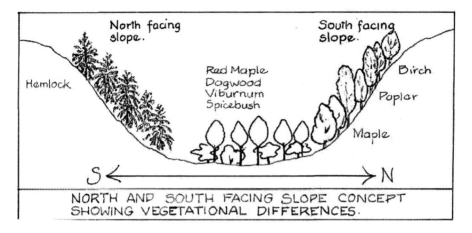

North facing slope. South facing slope.

Hemlock

Red Maple
Dogwood
Viburnum
Spicebush

Birch

Poplar

Maple

S ← → N

NORTH AND SOUTH FACING SLOPE CONCEPT SHOWING VEGETATIONAL DIFFERENCES.

Figure 4-3

Light is the other energy factor that has strong influence on plants. Certain wavelengths of the radiant energy spectrum we call light are critical for photosynthesis. For optimum growth the plant must get the proper wavelengths in adequate intensity for a long enough period each day and for a proper number of days each year.

Doing the kind of physical light measurements that precisely define a species' needs is a job for the plant physiologist in the laboratory. That does not mean, however, that the field observer cannot make practical observations about a plant's responses to light. The general effect of light is exerted on plants through changes in its quality, direction, intensity, and duration.

On a clear day the quality of sunlight in the open doesn't vary much in different habitats. There is some seasonal shift, however, due to differences in the distance that light waves must travel through the atmosphere. Thus, in winter more wavelengths in the red than in the blue end of the spectrum reach the earth. Clouds and fog also affect quality of light and these conditions can effect vegetation in areas where cloud cover or fog banks are present for extended period of time. Cloud cover, as a percent of sky obscured should be regularly noted in field journals. Fog, as the percent of the daylight hours it obstructs, should also be recorded.

Light intensity can be measured with photographic light meters that give a reading in foot-candle units. Although light intensity is changing quite constantly and is altered by passing clouds and other atmospheric event, we can get some useful general information using such meters. Use light reflected off a piece of white cardboard to secure consistently comparable readings at a site. Holding the meter a constant distance from the cardboard, take on reading in a open, unobstructed area and then take the rest of the readings at various sites in the habitat such as near a forest floor, at six feet, and at even higher locations if possible. Express each reading as a percentage of the light reading you got out in the open.

If a plant you are studying gets direct light part of the day and shade the rest, keep records of the hours or minutes that the plant gets direct light versus how long it gets filtered light. This light regime may determine where the plant has a chance to flower or only to grow vegetatively. Many northeast woodland forest floors have healthy-looking blueberry plants that no longer flower and fruit because the closing woodland canopy produces and inadequate light regime. Diffuse light tens to promote development of vegetative structure, while intense light favors development of flowers, fruits, and seeds. Thus the great flower extravaganzas are in field, deserts and tundras rather than in forests. Such floral shows as occur in forests generally appear in deciduous forest in early spring, before the leaf covers of the trees appears and shuts off much of the useful wavelengths.

Light intensity has a creative impact on leaf formation, and this is something the alert observer can see. Light affects *chloroplasts* in leaves and the cell that contain them. *Sponge parenchymal* cells tend to produce leaf growth at right angles to incidental light, thus creating a thin, broad leaf. This results in a leaf with more area to catch light waves. *Palisade parenchyma* cells, on the other hand, tend to extend the leaf in the direction of the incidental light, thus producing a thicker leaf. Even within a given tree you can see these adaptation. So-called *sun leaves* at the outer layer of the tree crown tend to be smaller and thicker while leaves inside the crown and on lower branches, *shade leaves*, will be thinner and broader. Examination with a microscope reveals a different predominance of sponge or palisade layers in those leaves. It is not surprising that plants of many species of sunny, dry habitats have small leaves with a preponderance of palisade cell, nor that aquatic plants, with submerged leaves that must deal with reduced intensity of light filtered through water, have predominately sponge cells in the leaves.

Plant species vary considerably in their tolerances to shade. Light is an important factor in this, but is linked to interconnected factors of temperature and soil moisture as well. Light's influence is greatest on seedlings. Some species are light-demanding and very intolerant of shade—for example, willows, sumac, bluestem grasses, cottonwood, jack pine, and lodgepole pine. Other species are very tolerant of shade—for instance, beech, sugar maple, basss-wood, and hemlock. The inherent tolerance of seedlings to shade will have considerable impact on the species' ability to invade and become established in new sites. Some shade-tolerant species, like beech and hemlock, may survive many decades of slow growth and suppression before a new opening in the canopy gives them opportunity for a growth spurt and a dominant place in the vegetation. The degree of shade-tolerance of a species also contributes to membership in the various layers of woodland. In many kind of healthy wood-land, there will usually be four reasonably distinct vegetation layer: the *herbaceous layer* at the forest floor composed of grasses, sedges other herbs and assorted non-flowering plants such as mosses and ferns; a *shrub layer* of shade-tolerant shrubs; and *understory* of young shade-tolerant trees; and the *canopy* of dominate trees which may or may not be species with shade-tolerant seedlings.

The chart below indicates some shade tolerances of common trees in North America:

Very Shade Tolerant intolerant	Shade tolerant	Shade
Sugar maple (*Acer saccharum*)	Elms (*Ulmus*)	Silver Maple (*Acer saccharinum*)
Beech (*Fagus*)	White Oak (*Quercus alba*) Red Oak (*Quercus borealis*)	Bur Oak (*Quercus macrocarpa*)
Basswood (*Tilia*)	Black Oak (*Quercus velutina*)	Poplar (*Populus}*
Yew(*Taxus*)	Ash (*Fraxinus*)	Willow (*Salix*)
Hemlock (*Tsuga*)	White Pine (*Pinus strobus*)	Ponderosa Pine)
Fir (*Abies*)	Douglas Fir (*Pseudotsuga taxifolia*)	(*Pinus ponderosa*)
White Cedar (*Thuja*)		Lodgepole Pine
Larch (*Larix*)		(*Pinus contorta*)

MOISTURE

You can get some idea of the varying shade tolerances of tree species by observing crown density, degree of self-pruning relative to height of growth, and growth of a young stand under the old. In light-demanding species, leaves are concentrated at the outer part of the crown, or the crown is open so all leaves get plenty of light. Shade-tolerant species will have much denser crowns. Shade-intolerant species will self-prune their limbs high up, even in open habitats, Self-pruning is the process of the leaves and branches dying and being removed by wind or gravity. Shade tolerant species will have leafy branches much closer to the ground and their stems will tend to be thick in proportion to their height By and large, shade-tolerant species cannot establish themselves in stands of their parents or of other shade-producing species. Shade-tolerant species will produce seedling beneath stands of adults of their species but these seedlings generally will not thrive.

MOISTURE

Essentially, all the physiological processes in a plant take place in the presence of water. Water is required for respiration, photosynthesis, and the transport of photosynthates throughout the plant. The plant also transpires quantities of water under most conditions, and water gives considerable support and rigidity to plants. Because of ongoing water loss through transpiration, growing plants must have access to fresh supplies from the environment, primarily from the soil. Water, and minerals dissolved in it, are often taken in through the roots with the aid of cellular extension called *root hairs,* which increase the absorptive surface. Other plants increase their roots' ability to take in moisture and nutrient by means of a symbiotic relationship with *mycorrhizal fungi.*

As we remarked earlier in the section on soils, the amount of water in the earth can vary considerably from only a thin film adhering to soil particles to total saturation of all available space between solid particles. Plants have a variety of adaptations for coping with their needs for water and its tendency to be available in amounts either too great or too small. Tolerances to excess or deficiency are highly varied according to species, but they tend to fall into three categories:

> Hydrophytes (from the Greek *hudor*=water and *phyton*=p1ant)
> Xerophytes (from the Greek *xeros*=dry and *phyton*=nplant)
> Mesophytes (from the Greek *mesos*=middle and *phyton*=planat)

Plants adapted for life submerged in water or floating are called hydrophytes. Some hydrophytes are actually amphibious, with parts submerged and parts emerging from the water, such as cattails. The major adaptations of hydrophytes deal with ways of increasing absorption of carbon dioxide, and neither water loss or intake mechanisms are emphasized.

Xerophytes, on the other hand, have many adaptations for taking advantage of such little moisture as becomes available and for conserving that moisture against excessive loss through transpiration. Mesophytes are less tolerant of moisture content extremes at either end of the continuum.

At their extremes, moisture preferences or tolerance among the apparent mesophytes are much subtler and should stimulate continuing observation and data gathering by plant watchers. Soil moisture record from a number of plant stations over time will help indicate the range of preferences and the responses of plants to unusual flooding or drought conditions. Flooding presets some unusual situation, so duration of the flooding should be noted. There are species that can endure moderate periods of annual flooding, but even these have distinct limits on how long they can remain inundated and survive. If you have an opportunity to study a newly flooded area, by a beaver dam for instance, you will be able to determine some of the tolerance limits. Even plant species that can stand periodic streamside flooding may eventually succumb to prolonged immersion behind a beaver dam.

For non-flooded conditions on most soils, you can gather data with electronic moisture meters available in many gardening and houseplant supply stores. These are not the most precise tools available, but they are suitable for rough field observations. Be sure to note the make and model of the instrument you are using for data gathering so its relative reliability can be ascertained later if necessary.

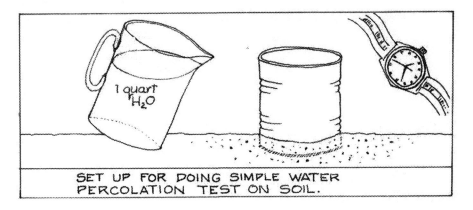

SET UP FOR DOING SIMPLE WATER PERCOLATION TEST ON SOIL.

Figure 4-4

INTERPRETING ENVIRONMENTAL INFORMATION

It would be so nice if only we could ascribe particular plant behaviors as responses to a particular environmental factor. In some cases, after long and careful laboratory study, this is possible; but in general the various environmental factors are so interrelated that it often is not possible to separate one factor as being most responsible. Reduced light induces stem elongation, while a shortage of phosphorous will prevent stem elongation. In some situations the two factors could cancel each other out as far as plant growth is concerned. Increased light intensity usually results in higher temperature. If a plant grows well under these conditions, which on is it responding to—light intensity or heat? Interpreting the relationships between a plant and its physical environment is seldom easy. It may take sophisticated mathematical analysis. What is clear, however, is that no analysis is possible without data to analyze.

As regularly as possible, plant watcher are urged to gather as much environmental data as they can about the local condition where the plants they are observing live. These data may appear to have little meaning at first, but as they accumulate you may begin to see some definite patterns or gain the statistical tools to mine the data for less obvious patterns. Data not collected are like fish that got away. A day may come when you wish you had certain information that you failed to collect and note for any of a number of reasons.

Even discovered patterns may raise more questions than they answer. However, the data may suggest some field or laboratory experiments that can provide more definite answers. It is partly the puzzles, dilemmas, and frustrations that give stimulation and added joy to the study of the endless diversity of the plant world.

5

A MATTER OF ASSOCIATES

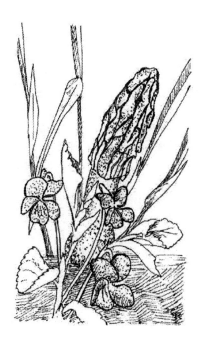

The alert observer walking about the countryside with an eye to the plants soon begins to notice that the different species are not randomly scattered across the landscape. To be sure, there may be places where many acres seem to be almost totally occupied by a single species, but even there closer examination will turn up a variety of other species in less abundance.

Extended observations will most likely reveal that wherever you spot species A, species B,C, and D are likely to be found close by. This may be because their basic needs are very similar, in which case they may be in direct competition for the same space and resources. On the other hand, they may have quite different adaptation that let them utilize different portions of similar habitat or tolerate the stresses one species places on another. Such a mix of species that share space, utilize slightly different resources, and perhaps depend on conditions created by other species such as various degrees of shade, may be thought of as a *plant community*.

Plant ecologist Henry Oosting offered as a working definition of community the following: "An aggregation of living organisms having mutual relationship among themselves and their environment." Mutual relations in this definition include both competitions between species and individuals and dependence of one species on another. The challenge to the plant observer is determining the nature and extent of the relationships between plant associates, and thus each associate's place in a designated plant community. WE must also be continually aware that a community includes animals and members of other life-kingdoms as well, and that through co-evolution these may play critical roles in the functioning of a community. For example, certain insects are critical to completion of plant life cycles through pollination and a number of bacteria species are essential for making available mineral nutrients for various plants. The plant observer is not likely to observe all of these things, yet he or she must remain aware of their presence and importance.

The first challenge to you as an observer of plant communities is to perceive a pattern of association. This involves making thorough lists of the species that inhabit a particular habitat you are studying or that you find within a specified radius of a particular species you are investigating. In doing this think three dimensionally, for there are vertical zones of occupancy as well as horizontal ones, and each zone has its own characteristic species that may influence the species in other zones. There will be time when you feel as though you are engaged in a game of three-dimensional tic-tac-toe. However, to the plants it is not a game it is life.

First gather information about which associates grow in a given local community or stand. Later compare them with what appear to be similar communities. Although there are broad areas of similarity, you probably will discover enough differences to raise serious questions about whether or not they are indeed the same types of community. At that point in your investigation, the tools of statistical analysis will have to be brought to bear on our data. It is beyond the scope of this book to explain the mysteries of statistics, so if you reach that stage seek someone at a local college or university to help you develop the needed statistical tools or to recommend available computer programs that can perform the appropriate tasks.

INFORMATION TO SEEK

As you assemble information about plant associates, you will need both quantitative and qualitative data. Quantitatively you need to find out how many of each species is present, their approximate size, and some measurement of how much space they occupy. Qualitatively you need to acquire data on how each species is grouped or spaced out within the community including its place in the vertical as well as horizontal layering. You will want to gather information on how each species develops through critical stages in its life cycle—that is, at what stages in the annual cycle of the community it is prominent. For example, many herbaceous plants of the northeast United States deciduous forest communities flower and die back before the tree canopy leafs out. Even though they might be completely overlooked in an autumn study, they are nonetheless part of those plant associations. Each species goes through several distinct periods throughout the year, such as a leafing—out period, a leafless period (for many at least), a flowering period, a fruiting period, and an embryo period. Timing and duration of these periods are part of the phenological records you can gather.

Appendix D explores the nature and use of quadrats and/or transects as tools to gather quantitative information from samples of the various plant associations. In exploring the use of these quadrats or transects you will gather quantitative data about the following:

Abundance of each species. Some people explore their study plots and develop a subjective estimate of whether a species is very abundant, abundant, infrequent, rare, or very rare. Except when you are traveling and lack time for careful accounts, this data is seldom of much value. The problem is that different observers vary in their perception of just how many must be present to meet a specific category. My "abundant" may be your "very abundant".

Occupance. The space a plant species occupies in a community is a strong indicator of its impact on that community and its relative dominance there. The larger the plants are the greater access they have to basic resources and the greater demands they make upon them. Data should be gathered on a species' place and occupancy in each vertical stratum present, as well as what is perceived while looking down from above the study plats. Serious plant watchers may also try to get some information on the soil occupancy of the various root systems because roots are important to a species' role in the community. Plants that dominate a community usually compete successfully at every level of the community.

As indicated in Appendix D, it is fairly easy to measure the crown area of at least the larger plants when working with quadrats. For grasses this is more difficult, but most people simply measure the circumference of the grass clump. This provides a reasonable measurement but does not adequately indicate the area shaded by the leaves. This shaded area impacts on which seedlings of tall herbs can become established there. For some forestry purposes, basal diameter of trees at breast height is used, but this measurement likewise ignores the impact of the crown area on shading and changing microclimates and also on the competitive action of the root systems. These statements ate not intended to confuse, but only to indicate that certain data, which are relatively easy to gather and do have some uses, must be employed carefully because they could lead to very misleading statements.

When examining vertical zones, map the area of cover for each appropriate height.on clear plastic sheets. Then superimpose the cover maps of these various heights one over the other, the combination may reveal causes of patterns on the ground.

Distribution Pattern. This information may best be gathered by mapping but can be entered descriptively in your notes. What this data tells is where plants are located in what sort of density. What it doesn't tell you is why they are so arranged. Patterns are seldom constant from one place to another, but there are definite tendencies for certain species to be distributed according to specific patterns because of their species-specific reproductive strategy or the distribution patterns of certain environmental factors, such as moisture or nutrients, which are critical to their survival.

Descriptive terms for distribution patterns of a species follow a rough continuum from wide dispersion to high gregariousness and include such terms as:

> *grows singly in small patches* (usually refers to individual, seed-generated plants);
> *small or large colonies* (usually refers to clonal groups, vegetatively reproduced);
> large groups (often cluster of patches);

mats (extensive cover of small plants, usually bryophytes and other non-flowering groups);
pure stands (fairly extensive areas of a single species).

Because it is prone to change, the distribution pattern of a species in a community should be checked with regularity. Change occurs because of alterations in local environmental conditions. Note should be taken of the maturity of the plants and their reproductive state since the distribution pattern of seedlings may vary significantly from that of established plants. Likewise, if a species reproduces by a vegetative strategy, its distribution pattern may also alter once its seedlings become established and vegetatively active. These things lead to the phenomenon of *succession*—that is, the replacement of one plant community by another over time.

COMMUNITY—WHO'S A MEMBER?

Even with good data, it is not always easy to determine whether or not the species you find associating with one another actually compose a community. It depends in large measure on careful definition of the characteristics use to verify membership in a particular community. Just as with human communities, some species get along and can and will mix with any community in which they find themselves. Others confine all their activities to a very limited neighborhood. There are also those who survive in a variety of settings, but can settle in and raise a family only in a particular type of community.

As you begin to look at samples of plant communities of any particular habitat, you need to determine from your notes the frequency with which each species occurs in mixed stands of that habitat. A basic scale for this is:

If a species appears in one to twenty percent of the stands, it is rare,
Twenty-one to sixty—percent occurrence marks it as often present,
Sixty-One to eighty—percent reflects it as mostly present,
Eighty-one to one hundred percent reflects it as constantly present.

But presence of a species in a habitat is not enough to confirm it as a bona fide member of that community. You need to determine over time how it develops in that place. It may be frequently present as seedlings but fail to become established, or it may even get established but fail to do well enough to complete its life cycle and reproduce. *It is the ability to complete its life cycle by reproducing sexually that is most often set as the criterion for true community mem-*

bership. There are even species that survive on a site and reproduce vegetatively but never sexually; such are often excluded as true members of that community.

As you compare different sets of plant associates to determine whether or not they represent the same, or at least very similar, communities, you will want to compare lists of the species present and also have some idea of these species' presence or absence in other nearby plant communities. Such comparison can be undertaken only after considerable time afield and the acquisition of a reasonably broad knowledge of the life histories of the component species.

For any community under study you will want to determine if a particular species is:

1. a stranger whose presence is essentially accidental

2. present here but also found in many other communities with no apparent preferences

3. a *preferent,* living in a number of communities but showing greatest success in this one.

4. a *selective,* found generally in this community but occasionally growing elsewhere.

5. an *exclusive,* found only in this type of community.

Not all communities have exclusive species, but for those that do, such species can be considered indicator species—that is, whenever you se the species you can identify the type of community. Selective and preferent species, along with any indicator species, comprise a community's characteristic species. If indicator species are lacking, you may not be sure what type of community those other plants represent. Resolve the question as to whether two communities are essentially of the same type or different, you may need to determine *the coefficient of community,* a mathematical expression of the degree of similarity of species lists for the two communities being compared.

To determine the coefficient of community, compare lists of species found in the two communities and note the number of species found on each of the lists. Next, find the total number of species in the combined lists. Divide the first number by the second to determine coefficient of community. Thus:

<u>Number of species common to A and B</u>=Coefficient of Community

Total number of species in A and B

The closer the coefficient approaches one, the greater the similarity and the greater the likelihood that they represent the same community. To refine the determination of the degree of similarity between communities is quite possible, but when you are ready to proceed, it is time to enlist the advice and assistance of a professional botanist or ecologist.

Up to this point you may be aware that we have not named any particular plant communities. That is because there is no commonly agreed-upon classification for them. Some ecologists refer to the according to their outstanding physical features, such as southern or northern bog community; others would use and indicator plant to identify the same communities, such as white cedar bog community or black spruce bog community. Others may classify according to several characteristic genera—i.e., beech-birch-maple forest, oak-hickory forest, or a bit more technically, the *Spartina-Juncus* tidal marsh.

Thus, the name for a community is a judgmental matter of preference. It seems most practical, however, to name communities by the two or three most characteristic genera or species and/or dominant physical characteristics, at least in temperate regions.

Because communities do not exist in a vacuum, ecologist have elaborate classifications for different degrees of community association. These associations are often called communities as well, with such broad headings as wetland communities, desert communities, tall grass prairie communities, short grass prairie communities, deciduous forest communities, coniferous forest communities, and alpine communities. Such units are composed of sub-units and each has common vegetational characteristics. However, they may vary considerably geographically in regard to their flora.

Every community is constantly undergoing change. The very presence and activity of the major species causes changes in the nature of the surroundings. Height relationships change, temperature conditions at various levels are altered, nutrients are added and depleted, space is occupied, and soil structure may be altered. The observant naturalist becomes aware of these changes, for they offer clues to the future of plant association at any particular site. It is with such studies that knowledge of a species' germination and establishment needs come into play, along with knowledge of vegetative reproduction habits.

In many associations the established plants so alter conditions that their own seeds have difficulty germination or getting established. On the other hand, these same conditions may be just right for other species to get established and in turn create totally unsuitable condition for continued survival of species that preceded them. As this happens and associates of these invading species also appear, the old community will slowly but surely be replaced by a new one. In time this new community will suffer a similar fate

The *succession* of one community by another will eventually reach a stage at which the physical conditions of the site are relatively stable for that climate. At that time, the species dwelling there are so adapted that their own offspring can become established on the site and fill any vacancies that may occur. Generally it takes well over a century of undisturbed community succession to reach such a state of relative equilibrium. Many ecologists call such a community a *climatic climax community*. Climate, of course, is the long-term average of weather condition, and it is assumed that this community is the vegetative pattern best adapted to those conditions. Thus it is the climax, or end product, of a sequence of communities.

Other researchers are less sure that this is the case. Within most regions topography makes pockets of alternate climates, and some of these are quite stable over periods of time considered long by human standards. Plant communities different from the supposed climax clothe these pockets. Similarly, outcrops of certain types of bedrock create soils that support unique vegetation islands within the supposed climax. The criterion is essentially one of time. The whole Earth is constantly changing, and many of these changes require a time frame outside the general comprehension of most of us. This means that the climate is always changing as well, and so too the vegetation patterns responding to it. Changes one thought to occur only over time periods of thousands of years are now being found to change within human life spans. Climate change is occurring rather abruptly. Rather than a concept that explains what is happening in the world about us, the concept of climax may only be a shortsighted intellectual device to satisfy the human desire to find order in nature.

WATCHING COMMUNITIES CHANGE

A good plant observer records what is actually happening, not what he or she expects to happen. Because nature is full of surprises, much of what has been written in the popular literature and textbooks reflects data from a relatively few cases and tends to present them as generalities. Such generalities may or may not hold true for the particular plant community you are investigating, so watch carefully, regularly, and keep careful journal records of what you observe.

Note what plant strangers begin to appear in you plant community and whether they become established. Many seedlings come and go; the important thing is which species gain a secure roothold. Carefully note where in the community they get their start. Was it an opening caused by some physical disturbance? Was it in the shade of an already established plant? Then note how the strangers expand their occupancy in the community. Is it by sending out tillers of some type? Is it by saturating the area with seeds? Is it by expanding their crowns and thus light-starving plants beneath them? All of these are strategies different plant species use to reach new sites, become established, and enlarge their occupancy of a site.

As one community is beginning to replace another, keep alert to whether certain of the characteristic species of the new community regularly arrive ahead of various others—theat is, are certain species "advance men" for the new community?

As you watch one community replace another, one thing becomes relatively clear. size is an advantage. At each succeeding stage, the major components of the community are generally those species with the largest life forms—these are the species that become dominant. These large individuals tend to put stress on their smaller neighbors by increasing their own access to the physical resources of the site—water, light, and mineral nutrients—and by reducing access to light, creating increased litter on the surface, and perhaps releasing chemicals into the soil that are toxic to other species.

SURVIVAL STRATEGIES

In recent years some plant ecologists have begun to look at the varying stressful conditions plants have to face and are discovering that there are various strategies that plants have evolved to cope with these situation. Details vary from species to species and determine a species' relative success with the strategy. However, there are commonalties among all species employing each particular basic strategy. These strategies have been well elucidated by the British plant ecologist J.P. Grime, and I owe a great debt to his work for the material in this section. Become alert to the strategies plants in you communities appear to be employing.

Any plant must face a potential of two great challenges: (1) difficulties in gaining access to one or more of the basic resources needed for its life processes, called *stress*; and (2) recovering from physical damage due to predation, hail, fire, trampling, mowing, and the like, called *disturbance*. Since they cannot relocate or avoid these challenges, plants have had to evolve various solutions and incorporate them into the very structure and life history.

Dr. Grime has postulated three major and four secondary types of survival strategies among established plants and five types of regeneration strategies. Plant observers should look for the characteristics of these strategies among the species under study and see what strategies are being used by each of the majority species involved in the transition from one plant community to another via succession.

Plants utilizing the three primary stages are referred to *as competitors, stress-tolerators,* and *ruderals,* and each is linked to a particular combination of the two challenges of stress and disturbance. Competitors function in situation of both low stress and low disturbance. Stress-tolerators function best in sites where stress may be high but disturbance is low. Ruderals function in situations where stress may be low but disturbance is high. There is no effective adaptation to situation where both stress and disturbance are very high. Such sites remain essentially barren of plant life

COMPETITORS

When neighboring plants attempt to utilize the same available light, the same particles of mineral nutrient, the same molecules of water, or the same volume of space, they are competing. Competitor species tent to show rapid leaf and root expansion, and lateral spread. They send shoots up rapidly and become tall, have good root storage to provide the energy for the rapid growth, and may have extensive branching rhizomes or tillers to occupy vacant areas rapidly.

Competitors respond to damage, such as defoliation, by speedily sending up new shoots and leaves or by sending out a number of tillers that the send up leaves. This is particularly noticeable in competitor grasses used in lawns and pastures. All in all, competitors' adaptations let them take advantage of the resources of their environment at a high rate. In productive, crowded habitats, those plants that can tap the highest amount of the available resources are favored for survival and expansion. Competitors are aggressive in expanding their absorptive surfaces, such as roots and leaves, and flexible in physiologically expending their photosynthates where they will increase absorptive surfaces to tap resources most effectively. Stresses—such factors as lack of moisture, mineral depletion, shade, and the like—prevent plants from making plant material. Geared for growth, competitors are exploiters of the environment rather than conservers. Their ability to compete is severely curbed under increasing stress, and they fare best in productive habitats.

STRESS—TOLERATORS

There are five major kinds of habitats where stress is prevalent—arid areas, arctic-alpine areas, shaded habitats, saline habitats, and nutrient deficient habitats. Plants that survive in such habitats may have quite different specific adaptation, yet they also share a number of adaptations in common.

Stress-tolerators are slow growers with long-lived organs. Many are evergreen. They may flower infrequently, and they have mechanisms that let them take advantage of temporarily favorable conditions. They have adaptations to conserve their photosynthates rather then rapidly expending the on growth as do competitors and ruderals. Growth among stress-tolerators tends to be intermittent, and they show much less diversity of form within a species.

Stress is not the only hazard stress-tolerators face; because they grow slowly, loss of foliage to plant-eaters can be very dangerous and cause considerable setback from which recovery is slow or nil. Consequently, many stress-tolerators have toxic or unpalatable leaves or protective spines

RUDERALS

The Latin word for rubbish is *rudus,* and thus the plants that grow readily among the rubbish of disturbed areas are called ruderals. The term is applied here to the strategies of plants adapted to areas of low stress but high disturbance—that is, they are adapted to cope with factors of partial or near total destruction that prevent the building of their biomass.

Ruderals are found in such disturbed habitats as beach drift zones, silt deposits from floods, exposed shorelines of ponds and lakes that dry up seasonally, trampled ground where hoofed animals or people or their vehicles are abundant, plowed land, desert areas that get a brief rainy season, and smaller disturbed spots such as ant hills, animal wallows, bird dusting spots and similar small, bare patches.

Flowering plants adapted to such sites of recurring and intense disturbance generally have an annual or short-lived perennial life cycle. By rapidly completing their life cycle and maximizing seed production, they are able to exploit those environments that can support rapid plant growth only intermittently and for relatively short time spans. Ruderals are short-lived even when they don't face disturbance. For the annual species, death comes to the parent plant right after seed production. See ripening is very rapid among ruderals and a flower cluster may contain both blossoms and ripe seeds.

Ruderals tend to respond to stress by converting their growth efforts from vegetative growth to flower and seed production. Whereas competitors and stress-tolerators might forego flowering under stress conditions, ruderals strive harder to produce at least a few seeds. Because the environment they thrive in is so unstable, the parent plant is destined for a short life under the best of conditions; therefore, ruderals sacrifice the parent to assure offspring.

This all begins to seem a bit more like armchair ecology than field botany, but it does offer clues as to what plant lifestyles to be alert for. In early succession stages, communities are likely to be composed heavily of ruderal strategists or stress-tolerators depending upon the conditions. In primary succession situations, where the substrate is bare rock, barren soil, or open water the first colonists will probably be stress-tolerators. Their tenure is likely to be long, but in time they will moderate the condition enough for some ruderals to join the community along with some stress-tolerators of less extreme capabilities. Their presence will eventually create condition that allow invasion by competitor species whose strategies often quickly eliminate the majority of the ruderals and suppress the stress-tolerators. Competitors tend to overexploit certain resources, thus creating new stresses that give newfound advantage to other types of stress-tolerators. Secondary succession, often based on human initiated disturbance of an area follows a similar pattern but more usually begins with ruderals.

FINER TUNING

The major strategies are linked to major habitats, and one does not have to spend much time afield to realize that there is a much broader spectrum of habitat types than just three. It should not be unreasonable then to expect that there is also a broader spectrum of strategies, probably made up of aspects of the three major ones. Such does seem to be the case. The successional patterns you see can be very important in this time of global warming where more southern species are pushing northward and northern species are retreating toward polar regions or moving further up on mountain slopes.

A species like ragweed (Ambrosia artemisiifolia), for example, has a long vegetative phase and puts up tall shoots. Where many ragweed plants are growing close together, the broad spread of their leaves will form something of a dense canopy over shorter plants—characteristicss of competitors. Yet the plant comes in on disturbed ground and is an annual that produces many seeds and dies—marks of the ruderals. Dr. Grime calls such species competitive ruderals. Competitive ruderals may be annuals, biennials or perennials. The perennials, like yarrow (*Achillea millefolium*), creeping buttercup (*Ranunculus repens*), or Canada thistle (*Circium arvense*), are adapted to recently, but not newly disturbed sites. Although they put out many short—lived vegetative shoots and vigorous rhizomes and stolons, they are soon excluded by taller, more consolidated perennial species.

Competitive ruderals generally have a longer period of vegetative growth before flowering than other ruderals and thus develop greater biomass. They also occasionally can exploit environments already occupied by perennial species by doing most of their growth during periods of the year when the impact of the more dominant species is restricted. This strategy seems best adapted to habitats of low stress and where competition is kept moderate because of disturbance.

Stress-tolerant ruderals are found in habitats with a moderate degree of both stress and disturbance. A characteristic of such habitats is that the stresses occur during the growing period of the plants. These are difficult conditions necessitating specialization. Such situations are found in the arctic, on mountaintops, in deserts, and in shallow or sandy soils that dry out quickly. Most such species are small annuals or short-lived perennials that do their growth and flowering in the cool, wet season. Most are of small size, have slow growth rates, and produce seeds that tend to be small and remain dormant over the dry summers. There are also species that survive the dry seasons underground as bulbs, tubers, and rhizomes and do their vertical growing in cool, moist seasons.

These strategies are not limited to flowering plants; many or our mosses and liverworts can also be classified as stress-tolerant ruderals.

There are many species that illustrate a capacity for lateral spreading and are vigorous perennials. They have competitive strategy traits, yet these species have longer life spans for their leaves, lower maximum growth rates, and highest shoot biomass in summer with a marked decline in winter. Such a pattern describes a number of species of grasses, sedges, and rushes that are classified as *stress—tolerant competitors*. There's is a strategy for habitats of moderate productivity or stress and very little disturbance. Many woody plants utilize this strategy, particularly those found in the latter stages of forest succession where resource depletion increases the levels of stress.

There are also definite tends to the types of changes that occur as a community and its environment change, but these changes are not completely predictable. Dry, *xeric* habitats, ten to become moister, more *mesic*; and wet habitats become dryer, more mesic; but these trends can be reversed by any of several environmental events. Habitats that are periodically disturbed do not necessarily produce the same sequence of plant communities each time there is a set back and repeat of succession processes. Thus, we repeat an earlier admonition: The plant observer must faithfully record what is happening, not what he or she expects should be happening. Nature does what it will do. People try to find patterns and order in that and attempt to predict what will happen under given condition. Sometimes the order truly does exist in nature; sometimes it exists only in the minds of humans,

Figure 5-1

WHO IS DOMINANT?

In any association of plants a few species re dominant and get the majority of the available resources. In general, you can recognize dominants by their greater height, lateral spread, and litter production. Different species will exert different degrees of dominance in different settings. For example a goldenrod species that is dominant in an old field my loose that dominance as young poplars and dogwoods become established. How does that occur?

The answer lies in the various regenerative strategies that plants employ. Each species has its own variation on the main themes, but there are two major possibilities: through vegetative offspring or by seeds or spores. Some species can use only the latter, a number can use both, and a few, like bamboo, mainly reproduce vegetatively, rarely resorting to seed production. Seed distribution modes have evolved along with germination patterns, and these comprise the various strategies. These strategies apparently have evolved as means by which juvenile stages in a species life history can tolerate, or foil, the potentially dominating impact of established plants on a site.

Vegetative expansion by the sending out of persistent tillers, rhizomes, stolons, runners, and the like is a very important strategy that presents a low mortality risk, because the offspring maintain a prolonged attachment to the parent. It is a particularly useful strategy where heavy litter, shade, or other factors make reproduction through establishment of seedlings very difficult. It is also useful where fire and other disturbances cause above ground setbacks; stored photosynthate below ground can reestablish new growth quickly. However, vegetative strategies are most prevalent in relatively undisturbed habitats.

The other regenerative strategies to be alert for are adapted to exploit disturbances of one sort or another. Their individual uniqueness is shaped b the nature and frequency of disturbances and the environmental settings in which they occur.

Wind Distribution. We are often aware of windblown seeds such as those of dandelions and cottonwoods. Although the seeds are produced in vast numbers, relatively few ever get the opportunity to germinate. The strategy of wind distribution is useful for reaching areas of large scale and unpredictable disturbance, such as eroded field, plowed areas, and formerly flooded river terraces. Many devices have evolved to exploit this strategy, ranging from minute size of seeds and spores to complex tufts to catch the breeze to winged extensions that increase lift and drift.

Seasonal Regeneration. Across a wide range of habitats there is predictable seasonal damage that each year creates bare ground or sparsely vegetated openings. Such openings are the result of seasonal droughts, flooding, grazing and trampling, and the like, and are generally re-colonized each year during the season that is most advantageous to the colonizers. In temperate zones, these seasons ten to be either spring or autumn; and each season stimulates its characteristic strategy.

AUTUMNAL REGENERATION

This strategy is most readily used in regions where rainfall is primarily a phenomenon of the cool season, as in Southern California. In such regions a predictable dry season usually precedes the rain, and the dry season tends to kill shallow-rooted species, thus creating small openings. The trampling of grazing animals creates further openings.

Seeds of species that will germinate in fall have been lying on the ground through the dry spell and quickly respond to the onset of moist, cool conditions. Seeds of species that use this strategy are able to germinate in light or dark and over a wide range of temperature. The seeds are comparatively large so that they have a good start towards successful establishment and the life cycle can be completed before the next recurring dry spell. Many grass species use this strategy. There are also some plant species that reproduce by *bulbils* that follow a similar strategy. Bulbils remain dormant over the dry spell and regenerate with the coming of cool, moist autumn weather

SPRING REGENERATAION

In many parts of the North Temperate Zone, particularly inland on the continents, any plant growth in fall and winter is heavily restricted by low temperature and the action of frost. Consequently, any recurring openings in the vegetation that become available during summer remain unoccupied until spring. Winter itself often adds bare patches through frost heaves and erosion from the melting of early spring snow.

Seeds that are to germinate in spring re adapted to that by a genetically programmed chilling period. If they do not get chilled for a minimum period of time, which varies by species from several days to several months, the seeds will not germinate. Usually the seeds take on water in the fall and then await their chilling period when temperatures must fall between 1 and 2 degrees Centigrade. One the chilling period is completed and temperatures rise somewhere above 10 degrees Centigrade, the seeds begin to germinate. The actual temperature needed, which is species-specific, generally causes germination to occur at a time when seedlings will encounter the most favorable condition that will give them a good opportunity to become established and complete their life cycle

Persistent Seed Banks. If, as a serious plant observer, you sample soil regularly, you will usually find a number of seeds of various species. Comparison with a labeled seed collection, or use of one of the few seed keys, will help identify them. If you sample an area regularly, you may note that the percent of your sample that represents any particular species enlarges and shrinks on a seasonal basis. Some species will show up throughout the year, and some will appear only seasonally for a relatively short period. The assemblage of all these seeds represents a soil's seed bank. Shrubs and perennial herbs are usually heavily represented in a seed bank, as are many ruderal species.

Dormant seeds remain viable for varied periods of time; some only a year or so, others for centuries. To get into the seed bank, seeds must become buried and all must have some mechanism to delay germination after the seeds fall so that they will have a chance to be buried. Most seed-bank seeds are quite small, so they get washed into cracks and crevices in the soil by rain or get buried by the activities of earthworms and other soil animals.

Dormancy of seeds in a seed bank may be set by one of two approaches. The first approach is *enforced dormancy*, in which seeds fall so late in the season that winter temperatures prevent germination. The second is *genetically determined dormancy*, which sets chill requirements of demands an extended incubation period in warm, moist conditions for the embryo to mature. Other innate mechanisms to enforce dormancy include inhibition of germination by light and heavy, impermeable seed coat that must be mechanically nicked or burned off before it can take on water to germinate.

Once seeds are buried, opposite factors may enforce dormancy, a major one being inhibition of dormancy by darkness. The seeds will then remain in the seed bank until conditions are right for their germination. Such conditions usually result from some disturbance to soil or established vegetation above the seed bank.

Two factors seem to stimulate germination of buried seeds—penetration of light and/or increased daily fluctuations in soil temperature. These can occur due to gaps in the canopy or removal of the litter, or humus, that acts as and insulating blanket over the soil. Fire, windstorms, or other disturbances can bring this about.

I like to think of this response of seed banks as natural photography. When light penetrates through holes in the canopy, or in a clearing mad by man, the seed bank responds much as the silver iodide crystals to on photographic film. In creased temperature causes this seed film to develop into a "picture," which is the resultant mosaic of seedlings.

Seedling Banks. In mature forests, seeds of most species germinate a short time after they fall. However, under the condition they find, their growth after germination is very slow. Most of the seeds are comparatively large, and this undoubtedly helps the seedling survive until their roots and leaves are well established. These seedlings are generally quite hardy and persist over long periods of time. They grow very slowly and suffer many setback until some disturbance among the established trees creates and opening and thus opportunity for rapid growth. The challenge then is for the seedlings to marshal resources and grow upward fast enough to occupy the opening before surrounding trees extend enough laterally to close the opening. James P. Jackson in his Biography of a Tree, gives an accurate and dramatic view of this regenerative strategy and its challenges.

SUMMARY

Developing familiarity with the processes and strategies of plant communities and with succession provides years of challenging exploration. We have presented here, with a broad brush, overviews of such processes and strategies when they are really often quite subtle, crying for detailed treatment. Nonetheless, the average plant observer can begin to gain familiarity with them, particularly if he or she gains increased understanding of the life histories and phenology of more and more species that comprise various plant communities.

Those observers who find themselves confined close to home may not get a chance to see all the weird and wonderful plant species of faraway places. However, by detailing lives of local plants and t heir various associates and recording subtle changes in local environments, plant species, and the communities that result, plant watchers have much to stimulate them throughout their lifetimes.

Overall, it should be remembered constantly that plants are reacting to and responding to the immediate environment. The avid plant watcher must be as alert to the nature and changes in that environment as to the plant itself. Plant and environment are so intimately intertwined and interrelated that they become almost as one

II

LEARNING SPECIFICS THROUGH GUIDED NATURE JOURNALING

6

FOR THE
RECORD

There is much to be said for quiet walks through field, forest, mountain meadow, or desert draw to enjoy the various beauties of the vegetation and revitalize the inner spirit Under such conditions the only record necessary is that etched in the deep recesses of human memory. Detail is unimportant—only the broad impact on the emotions and spirit need to be recalled, the sense of mood engendered.

However, if you want to go beyond such generalities and for any purpose retrieve details of field observations and experiences hours, days, or years after they have happened, it is important to develop the skill and habits of journaling, that is the keeping of notes and records. A serious amateur botanist is always accompanied a field journal. This is simply a notebook that holds a continuous record of your field excursions and the observations you have made. It often becomes a treasured companion in the field. Entries are normally a blend of words and sketches but may included pressed leaves or other preserved plant parts, or photos you have taken and pasted in.

THE FIELD JOURNAL

A field journal can be a rather informal memory-jogger used to recall pleasant and stimulating observation when you are stuck at home during inclement weather or when for some other reason you can no longer go afield. Or it can grow into a more disciplined record of you observations and studies serving as a data base for your longer-term plant studies. It may also be used as a valuable resource for others.

Some basic conventions are useful. Each journal entry should carry the date, a description of the geographic location of the observation site, and general observations on the weather. It is also useful to make note of any others that may have accompanied you on the field excursion. (They may be helpful at a later date in cross-checking some fact from their own notes.) After such standard information, enter your observation about the plants of the site; these might include lists of species, notes on growth, phenological information, plant/animal interaction, ecological data, and related matters.

Description of the geographic location is very important if you, or someone else, are to relocate a site years later to determine if certain species are still there. It should be done precisely the initial time you visit a particular site. Record not only the broad indication of town, county, and state, but also present careful road direction and/or geographic coordinates from the appropriate topographical map. Such detail is consumptive of time and space, and we all quickly rebel at writing up a description for each visit to the same site. Instead, assign a number to each site at the time you prepare its first detailed description. This number is used as the site descriptor on each subsequent return along with a parenthetical note as to where the original description occurs in you series of journals (i.e. Locale #46—see Field Journal3, page 15. This site number can also be attached to the labels of any voucher specimens collected or on soil samples, photographs, or other pertinent materials.

If you are computer literate and are willing to invest in hand held global positioning equipment you can get accurate site readings and make maps on the computer locating each special plant you have observed.

Few people are guilty of taking overly detailed notes. Record as much information as you can at any particular location. Some of the information may seem irrelevant at the moment, but at some later time, as you ponder the data you have gathered, you may discover and apparent correlation that seems important. It is most frustrating to go back through older notes to locate additional supportive data only to find that you didn't bother to record any comparable information at all. Try to think of the particular plant not by itself but in its context. Describe its habitat, locale, plant and animal associates, altitude, exposure, soil conditions, and any other information that might possibly be influencing the plant's growth, health, and well-being. This is a difficult discipline to foster in the field, because there is often so much of interest happening that it seems a shame to "waste time" with extensive note taking. It normally takes several frustrating searches through one's not for essential but ultimately nonexistent prior detail to bring about the mental "knuckle-rapping" that fosters better detailed note-taking.

One way to increase detail in the notes is to use a standardized checklist of data to be gathered at each site. These checklists can be photocopied sheets that are carried afield on a clipboard and bound in with the descriptive field notes when completed. Also, take photographs that help give a good overview of the place and its plants. Sketch maps of the area indicating major plant communities, rock outcroppings, waterways, and the like can augment these photos. Plant observers have an advantage over wildlife observers because their subjects of study stay put and cannot flee from view while you are taking note

CHOOSING A FIELD JOURNAL FORMAT

Choice of the best format for a field journal is largely a matter of personal preference. Your style of note-taking is the primary determinant. Those who confine note-taking primarily to words generally prefer some form of lined pages. Spiral-bound notebooks appeal to many because the open flat and are easy to use in the field. However, pages can tear loose relatively easily and data may become lost. Others prefer stitch-bound books such as the journals available in many stationery stores. Because the will not open flat, they are more awkward to use afield, but they are generally of better quality with more durable paper not easily torn from the book. Those, like myself who like to use many sketches and maps in note-taking prefer the unlined pages and stitch-bound format of artists sketchbooks. These give good flexibility of style of recording, but they share the inconveniences of the aforementioned stitch-bound journals.

Keep the following points in mind when making your own choice.

1. Because your notes will probably be kept for many years and indeed may pass on to succeeding generations, choose a good quality paper. Acid papers slowly turn yellow and brittle with age; so when possible, choose rag papers. They are more expensive, but they will stand up to the years much more effectively.

2. Be sure the binding is durable. Stitch bindings, and plastic or steel spiral-bound notebooks are usually a good investment. Should you decide to use three-ring spring binders, be sure to reinforce holes in the pages with gummed rings to help prevent loss of good material.

3. Choose a size that fits conveniently into a coat pocket or day pack. A widely used size is 6"x9". I find that is a good size also for carrying in the belt packs designed for carrying field guides. I usually carry one field guide and my field journal in such a belt pack.

4. If you don't use a belt pack, make some form of waterproof covering to protect you journal from the vicissitudes of the weather and accidental drops into dew-covered grass, ponds, and the like. You may want to make the cover of vinyl or similar materials, or simply stuff the field journal into a self-locking plastic bag that can also serve as a spare specimen holder (*vasculum*) on occasion.

5. Almost as important as your choice of field journal is you choice of writing instrument. Its marking material must be waterproof and permanent. There is little more frustrating than seeing good notes dis-

solve into unintelligible streaks when hit by rain from a sudden squall or retrieved from a visit to a puddle.

Choosing Writing Instruments

Some people take all their notes in pencil because it doesn't run like inks may. But soft graphites such as the normal #2 and #2B are apt to smudge and the points wear down quickly. Harder graphites such as #2H and HB resist smudging and are slower to wear down, but the line they leave is light and harder to read. Most of those who prefer graphite choose a mechanical holder rather than a wooden pencil and carry plenty of spare "leads".

Many journalists like to carry a set of colored pencils. These allow them to make colored sketches of the plants which can be very useful in recording various aspects of the plant or making special word notes they want to stand out from the rest.

Ballpoint pens can be used if you are certain of the water-proofness of their inks. Purist insist that only a good waterproof India ink is appropriate for field notes; they prefer a fountain pen with Higgins Eternal or Higgins Engrossing ink. My preference is for a Rapidograph or Castell Drawing Pen filled with one of the newer, non-clogging drawing inks. Nonetheless, I always carry a pencil to use in damp or wet weather, or if the pen runs out of ink.

Your field journal is the heart and soul of you records of experiences afield. It is worth investing in the best materials you can afford and taking adequate time for note-taking and filing. Keep your journals on your shelves in numerical order and labeled with the first and last dates in each volume. This will help you refer quickly back to past observations. Keep notes clear and legible with food reference keys to abbreviations you habitually use; you never know who else may have reason to use your data in the future. If notes are legible only to you, their usefulness will be greatly impaired and, unless you keep a good key to each abbreviation, even you may forget exactly what your symbolic shorthand meant.

DEVELOPING SPECIES FILES

Your field journal is a valuable chronological record of your excursions but is often difficult to back to past specific entries containing notes on a particular species upon which you want to concentrate at some specific time. Maintain a second set of records into which each species' information is transcribed from the field journal.

One method is to record the information on file cards that can be filed by family, genus, and species. Be sure to note the page in the field journals from which each entry is transcribed so you can quickly check the accuracy of a transcription if need be.

Another format uses three-ring notebooks as its basis. This has the advantage that the field notes, plastic storage pages of slides and/or photographic prints taken, along with voucher specimens in plastic sleeves can all be kept together. As you become more deeply involved you may wish to devote a separate three—ring binder to each family or genus upon which you are concentrating. This method allows the detailed compilation of plant life histories as we suggested in Chapter 2. You can buy plastic storage sleeves for slides and prints from most large photo supply stores. Plastic sleeves or Mylar sheets to cover and protect voucher specimens can be found in stationery stores or can be ordered from biological supply houses. To include voucher specimens in this format will require some modification of conventional herbarium sheet sizes as noted below, but it is generally worthwhile.

VOUCHER SPECIMENS FOR THE RECORD

Collecting and pressing plants for a herbarium was a primary activity of botanist in past years; indeed it still is for many. During the age of exploration it was a valuable activity but it has more limited value today except under special situation that are primarily within the realm of professional botanists.

However, in many places you may undertake observations of a plant that you cannot readily identify or whose determination by you others may question. In such situations collect and prepare a *voucher specimen* of the species to include with your records. A voucher specimen is simply a good representative of the plant form upon which you are making detailed observation. Botanist may change their opinion about the appropriate name to assign a given species, subspecies or variety, but as long as you have the voucher specimen among your records all your data can be accredited to the proper taxon at any future time.

Although many identification books concentrate on a few features of the plant such as flowers or leaves, in preparing a voucher specimen you should collect the entire plant of small herbaceous species whenever possible. leaves, stems, roots, and flowers or fruiting bodies.

The plants can be gathered in the field and assigned a small tag or tape with a *field collection number*. This number is also entered into the field journal as well. Field collection numbers are sequential and begin with your first voucher specimen; they should never be repeated or confusion would reign! However, all specimens of the same species from the same site receive the same number. The tagged specimen should be kept moist until you are ready to press it. This can be done by carrying it in a standard botanical metal *vasculum* lined with damp newspaper or paper towels or by carrying it in a plastic bag. Treat the materials gently to keep damage to a minimum.

PREPARING VOUCHER SPECIMENS FOR THE LONG HAUL

Once you return home or to your base camp, begin the drying and pressing process. If necessary, larger plants should be folded into and N or M shape so that when dry they will fit onto an herbarium sheet. Standard herbarium sheets are 14"x16", but you may whish to cut them into an 81/2" x 11" size that fits in a standard three-ring binder. Care should be taken to lie out leaves and flowers carefully so that all possible detail can be readily observed. Prepared plants are placed between folded sheets of newspaper and then sandwiched between to dryers of blotter material, corrugated cardboard, or professional botanical dryers. These in turn are placed between the rigid wooden frame of the plant press, and pressure is applied by tightening straps or wing nuts depending upon the type of press used.

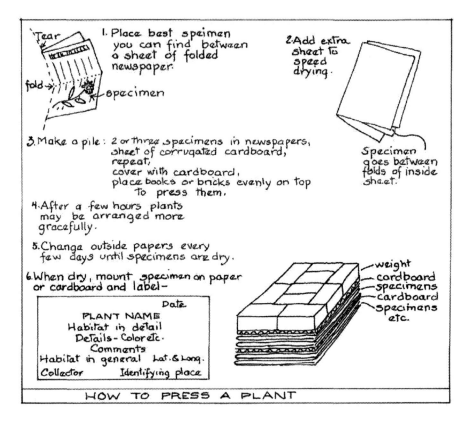

1. Place best specimen you can find between a sheet of folded newspaper.

Tear

fold→   specimen

2. Add extra sheet to speed drying.

Specimen goes between folds of inside sheet.

3. Make a pile: 2 or three specimens in newspapers, sheet of corrugated cardboard, repeat, cover with cardboard, place books or bricks evenly on top to press them.

4. After a few hours plants may be arranged more gracefully.

5. Change outside papers every few days until specimens are dry.

6. When dry, mount specimen on paper or cardboard and label—

Date
PLANT NAME
Habitat in detail
Details - Color etc.
Comments
Habitat in general Lat. & Long.
Collector   Identifying place

weight
cardboard
specimens
cardboard
specimens
etc.

HOW TO PRESS A PLANT

Figure 6-1

Dryers should be changed each day and replaced by fresh ones. Those removed can be place in the sun or other appropriate place to dry out for reuse. After a week or so in the press, the specimens should be adequately dry for permanent mounting unless the are unusually fleshy and/or succulent. Thick roots, tubers, and rhizomes should be sliced longitudinally to make them thinner while still reflecting their original shape and orientation.

Dried and pressed specimens are laid out on the final herbarium sheet and arranged a neatly as possible. Stems can be held in place with strips of transparent tape, but such tape will deteriorate far more rapidly than the plant material and in a matter of only a few years, the specimens will come loose from the backing sheet. Some people spread white glue on a sheet of glass and then lay their specimen on the glue. Next, the specimen with its coating of glues is carefully lifted off the glass and laid carefully, glue side down, on the herbarium sheet. If you are likely to prepare a number of specimens, apply Archer's solution as your adhesive in simple strips using a plastic catsup dispenser or an oil gun. Archer's solution is an efficient, neat, easily applied adhesive available from some biological supply houses.

If you use standard herbarium sheets, you will want to keep the finished specimen in an herbarium folder. If you use the 81/2"x11" size, enclose the finished specimen in plastic sleeves.

Whatever its format, an herbarium sheet must have a specimen label: unlabeled specimens are virtually useless scientifically. A label should contain:

> Field Collection Number
> Location:
> Date:
> Collector
> Species determination when possible
> Species determination by:_____

It takes work to prepare a good botanical specimen for your voucher records or for a formal herbarium. Take the time to do the job the way a craftsperson would. A specimen, properly prepared and stored, can be useful for hundreds of years.

RECORDING WITH A CAMERA

Plants are ideal for photography because there is plenty of time to set up the equipment and take good pictures. The major difficulty is coping with wind and the blurring it may cause. Photographing flowers is a hobby in and of itself. Nonetheless we are interested here in photographic records of plant activity although there is no reason why a record shot cannot be aesthetically pleasing and artistic even though record shots do not have to be so.

It is not the purpose of this book to go into detail about plant photography but we do want to make some suggestions about useful equipment. In general you are best using a single lens reflex camera with interchangeable lenses. This can be either a regular film camera or a digital one. There are also some fixed-focus cameras that are reasonably inexpensive and which are designed for close up work by dentists and the like. They come with built in flash and a focal frame attachments. The director of a nature center, an old friend of mine, uses such a camera to record every species of he finds blooming in his sanctuary.

This has provided a record of the plant life over the years without disturbing the plant's life history in any way. His collection of thousands of slides and prints provides an unparalleled record of the sanctuary flora by someone who detested the complex paraphernalia—tripods, lenses, flash units and the like—of the ardent photographer but who wanted good pictures nonetheless.

Because of the generally low angle desirable for much plant photography, it is helpful to get a camera with a waist-level viewfinder or a close focus frame attachment.

If you are interested in photographing underwater plants you will need a camera with some form of underwater housing. Today you can purchase single-use underwater cameras at many drug and camera stores for very little money.

TRIPODS

For clear sharp photographs a sturdy tripod is an essential piece of equipment. A low camera angle is desirable for photos of most plants, Ideally you are looking for a tripod that will let the camera get down to at least 18" or lower. If you can't find such a tripod, you can mount the pivoting head of a tripod on a wide flat board as illustrated here.

USEFUL SPECIAL PHOTOGRAPHY TECHNIQUES

Two special techniques of particular value to plant observers are time-lapse photography and ultraviolet photography. Time lapse work requires the use of a movie camera or video camcorder that can be advanced one frame at a time. Instead of passing by the camera lens at the standard rate of sixteen frames a second, film is put through at the camera at the rate of one frame per hour, or whatever time rate you determine as appropriate to the subject. However the developed fill will go through the projector at sixteen frames per second, resulting in the illusion of apparently rapid uncoiling of a fiddlehead fern, opening of a flower, grasping of a tendril, and the like. This technique is particularly useful in keeping track of the movement behavior of plants which occurs at a much slower rate than most animal behavior. Follow the day-long opening and closing of flowers, the thigmotropic responses of insect-eating plants, climbing plants, and sleeping leaves.

Ultra violet photography requires use of a special film sensitive to that part of the light spectrum and special lighting techniques, but the result is very revealing about flower patterns. Flowers that appear white to us may present distinctive patterns in ultraviolet, and many insects, particularly pollinators, are able to see in that spectral range. It is worth photographing flowers with ultraviolet film to determine how they may appear to such creatures.

FIELD SKETCHING

The advantage of photography is that the resulting picture is a remarkably detailed representation of the original object as it existed at that moment in time. It is not always possible, or even desirable, to take a camera afield, and carefully done field sketches are the next best thing. Sketches also require close observation of the object and the sketch can show a plant part drawn in a perspective or view that best shows key features. This is often not possible with the camera.

Field sketching also focuses observations, helping the observer see details that might normally have gone unnoticed—exactly how does the leaf attach to the stem; where are buds located; how is the flower placed? Some people are shy about sketching, but they needn't be. Like other skills, it develops only through practice. First and foremost, sketching is dependent upon seeing. Once able to truly see, you can learn some conventional ways to represent the illusion of three dimensions on a single plane using lines and shading. Over time you learn more refinements for building the illusions and become increasingly skillful.

Field sketching allows you to go afield lightly encumbered yet return with detailed notes and records of what you have seen. You will not have to transport extensive equipment to be set up over and over, nor worry about focus, exposure, angle and the like. You need only open your journal, observe carefully, and represent those observations in line, shading, and explanatory notes. The relative immobility of plants is a great asset to botanical field sketching and allows you to take adequate time both for observing and checking the accuracy of your representation. If you find an error, you have ample time to erase and redraw. Wildlife sketchers seldom have the luxury of such prolonged observation. Plant photographers often get so involved in the photographic process that they do much less close observation of the plant.

When sketching in the field journal, artistic rendering is not the primary purpose; more important is the accuracy of particular key features, such as the angle at which leaves emerge from the stem; how the lip of the flower orients to the horizon; the pattern of "toothed edges" on the leaves; the pattern of overlap of bud scales; and the like.

If you are having trouble with the accuracy of your freehand sketching, there are a variety of shortcuts you can take that are perfectly acceptable. For example you can put a leaf under the journal page and the rub over it with the side of the pencil to get an image that shows details of the leaf edge and venation.

Or you may want to carry a pane of window glass its edges covered with masking tape for safety, or a sheet of Plexiglas or Mylar, along with a glass marking pencil. If you are having trouble getting the appropriate outline of a tree and its branching or the precise perspective of a curling leaf, hold the glass pane in front of you at a constant distance and trace the outline of what you are viewing with the grease pencil. To change the size of the drawing, move the pane closer or further away from the object you want to draw. After drawing on the glass, the image can be traced, freehand copied, or copied by the proportionate square method into your journal. Wipe off the pane, sharpen the grease pencil and you are ready for your next venture. This approach is only a crutch, and people usually wean themselves away from it rather quickly.

HOW TO DRAW ON GLASS IN ORDER TO KEEP PERSPECTIVE ACCURATE WITH HINT OF PROPORTIONAL SQUARE METHOD WHICH WILL BE ILLUSTRATED LATER.

Figure 6-2

FIELD MAPS

The location of individual plants, or stations where a number of plants of a given species can be found is important botanical data. Much data can be recorded on simple, careful sketch maps in the field. The location of stands of a species, the approximate area of a tract inhabited by several different species, the patterns of seed or seedling dispersal, and the relationship of plant locations to geographical features can be recorded effectively on field maps along with other valuable data.

At a minimum you need a compass and measuring device along with you journal to produce such maps. The simplest type of map is a sketch map representing a particular area and upon which various items are roughly located. Essentially picture of relationships, such maps are abstract approximations with little attention paid to scale, distance, or geological orientation. They sometime are useful in presenting a very broad brush picture of a place or situation.

A more accurate depiction of the same area would require compass points and distances. These can be noted by a compass reading at a given point, an arrow to indicate direction, and a distance figure.

You can use a traditional compass rose notation such as NNW or, as I prefer, a Silva system compass with degree readings (azimuth). For reconnaissance work, distance can be determined by your pace. In determining the length of your pace, use a normal easy stride that you can maintain without significant change over a reasonable distant. For more accurate work, you will need a measuring tape.

Data can be entered in your field journal as a list and be converted to a pap at a later date. Such data might appear as follows:

From big rock to lone pine 32 degrees and 89 paces
From lone pine to willow shrub, 60 degrees and 95 paces
From willow shrub to dead pine snag, 190 degrees and 110 paces
From snag to sugar maple 225 degrees and 80 paces
From sugar maple to big rock, 330 degrees and 90 paces

Given your normal pace, you can convert the data to feet or meters at a later date when the map can be drawn more accurately to some appropriate scale. Within the area circumscribed by your map, you can locate various items by degrees and paces from you landmarks. To pinpoint them exactly, you will want to use two heading and the objects should be located where lines from the two headings intersect—i.e. ladies tresses growing in open grass area 40degrees and 85 paces from big rock, 70 degrees and 30 paces from lone pine. Such data can prove very handy when later trying to relocate stations of particular plants.

If you construct your map later, be sure to indicate on it the journal number and observation number where the original data can be located. Add a note in the journal that the finished map exists and where it is filed.

MARKING INDIVIDUALS

As you locate individual plants and plant stations on your maps, you may also want to mark them in the field with tags or markers that will help you relocate them later. A specimen easy to recognize in flower may look quite different at other times or may wither and disappear after flowering. A variety of materials may be used as markers, however all must have similar properties. They must be weather resistant, durable, relatively inexpensive, easy to handle, and easy to mark with an indelible marking pen. I have found the embossing label devices with their many colors of plastic tape very useful. With them you can punch out any name, number, or other code on a strip and then attach it to a sturdy part of the plant with florists' wire. With annuals, I mark the site using plastic markers that horticulturists stick in their pots to indicate species; the same is done with herbaceous perennials that die down below ground level. These labels can be written on with grease pencil or indelible laundry markers. There is always a certain amount of loss due to the activity of people and animal or machinery trampling, but these methods generally work quite well. If your maps are carefully and accurately prepared, you can easily relocate lost individuals.

F or some inconspicuous species in relatively undisturbed places, I may also use a more conspicuous marker such as a pole stuck in the ground with a piece of colorful surveyor's tape tied to it. These are consistently set at a specific distance and direction away from the marked plants so that curiosity seeker do not inadvertent trample on the plants as they investigate the markers.

JOURNAL DATA AND THE COMPUTER

With the reasonable affordability of home computer, more and more amateurs are likely to consider storing at least some of their field data in their home computer where it can be retrieved quickly for various forms of analysis. Developing skill to do the necessary programming is well beyond the scope of this book, but there are factors about the data-gathering process that are appropriate to consider here.

The less organized the data is that is entered into the computer, the greater will be the difficulty of retrieving and analyzing it. Unorganized data requires more complex programs and capacities for analysis than the basic home computer can supply. This doesn't mean you can't use your computer, it simply means that you should do very careful advanced planning before entering the information into the machine. In fact, that planning should usually take place even before the data is collected.

In keeping a field journal as an amateur, you generally collect a series of more or less random observations about a variety of interesting things that you come upon in your botanizing rambles. In time, some particular question about plant life may begin to occupy your mind and focus your observations. It is at this point that the potential of computer may well enter into the picture. You will begin to compile larger and larger amounts of comparable data that you want to analyze for a potential answer to your question. This is the forte of the computer—arranging, rearranging, and analyzing COMPARABLE data toward some predetermined objective. You may want to discover the frequency with which given sets of plant species associate, or perhaps, how consistently annual growth rates of particular species match with rainfall, or any of thousand of other objectives.

Different kinds of questions require different sets of data for analysis—that is, they require different data structure. Unfortunately, the data structure that is appropriate for one particular set of objectives may be quite inappropriate for others. Thus you must first establish your questions and objectives to determine the appropriate data structure. From that structure you can design data-collection forms that will speed your data collection by standardizing terms, assuring comparable data from different stations, and providing format for reasonably error-free transfer from field data to computer storage. In designing data structure, considerable though should be given to ways of accessing data to meet your analytical need and any application of data needs.

This will also help you decide what available computer programs you should acquire to do the work.

In collecting data for computer use, you will want to violate one of the precepts of field observation—that is, instead of gathering as much data as possible, you will want to limit your data collection only to those data that contribute directly to the objective. You will concentrate on a standardized format for data gathering as suggested above. (Note: This does not preclude collecting other observations in your journal)

SHARING OBSERVATIONS AND DATA

Knowledge gained is not only and individual possession but, where possible, should become part of humanity's aggregate knowledge. There are several ways this can be done. The simplest is through direct sharing as a participant in botanical and natural history organizations such as clubs and nature centers. Such groups provide opportunities to learn from perhaps more experienced others, and a responsive group who also want to hear of your experiences, discoveries, and hypotheses.

As you go about your exploration you may assemble a respectable collection of herbarium specimens, photographs, and field notes. It is farsighted to talk to officials at museums, herbariums, state natural heritage programs or universities about potential arrangements for accessioning you material when you die. Any such arrangements should be discussed with your loved ones so they will know how the materials should be dealt with. Such preplanning will assure that the information continues to contribute to our overall knowledge and that both institution and family are aware of the extent and value of "that silly hobby".

At some point you may even want to share some of your information in a magazine or journal article or by giving talks at garden clubs nature centers, and the like..

Keeping a Nature Journal is basically a free-spirited endeavor. The journalist goes into nature and comments in writing, or by drawing those things that catch the person's attention. As one observes he or she becomes aware of ever more detail and interest and proceeds at one's own pace. It is fun and can be quite productive.

With Guided Nature Journaling one is trying to generate information and understanding about a particular thing. In this case, plants. Since exploring the lives of plants may be quite a new venture for the journalist, he or she may be somewhat lost about what kind of things to observe

In this book I have tried to set up a set of guides that help the beginner get started. Like basic Nature Journaling it is still approached in a free—spirited manner but the left hand Column of the pages in this section suggests some of the things to look for. I emphasize SOME, there are many other things that may come to your attention and these should be recorded.

The methods you use to capture your observations, writing, drawing, photography are purely up to you. A combination will ultimately probably be best depending on your confidence with the different formats. If you intend to use some photographs be sure to leave room on the pages to paste them in later when they have been developed and printed..

BEGINNING YOUR GUIDED JOURNALING

The pages in the following section are set up to allow you to use this book to begin your actual journaling. When you have run out of space you can get blank books and continue your observations noting the dates covered on the cover of each completed book.

To help you get started in keeping journal records of your encounters with plants we have created the following templates to guide your observations. Each template consists of a left hand column of Things To Look For or Things to Do and a right hand space to record your observations. In fainter type face, which you can write over, is a quote to stimulate your thinking and reflection. These template pages are followed by some blank pages for each template for you to continue your note taking until you set up your own journal to continue your pursuit of information about plant lives through ongoing observations.

The different template sheets in this section are arranged from basic observation of individuals to more involved observations on populations, special plant groups, or more narrow aspects of a plant's life history. We do not cover all aspects of a life history with these templates. Once you have the idea you can go on to build your own observation templates using questions in the Life History Outlines which immediately follow the template section. For more general information on nature journaling see:

NATURE JOURNALING or (KEEPING A NATURE JOURNAL, 2nd
edition)
by Clare Walker Leslie and Charles E. Roth., Storey Publishing 2000

I wish you great success as you launch into this venture, and hope the effort
you will find richly rewarding for a lifetime.

7

SOME GUIDED JOURNALING PROJECTS

BUILDING LIFE STAGE OBSERVATIONS

THINGS TO LOOK FOR ABOVE GROUND	
SEEDS	
•shape	
•size	
•color	
INFANCY	
seed leaves (cotyledons)	
•size	
•shape	
•color	
•longevity	
sprouts form below ground	
•shape	
•growth pattern	
•number of leaves	
JUVENILES	
first true leaves	
•shape	
•size	
•texture	
•longevity	
ADOLESCENCE	
How many leaves?	
Pattern of leaves on stem	
•alternate	
•opposite	
•spiral	
Maximum height	
MATURE PLANTS	
flowers	
•size	
•shapd	
•color	
•placement on plant	
•number per plant	
growth habit	
•climbing	
•bushy	
•erect	
•recumbent Stems	
•hairy	
•fuzzy	Plants are extraordinary…Now two plants are alike…I start
•smooth	with the seedling, and I don't want to leave it. I don't feel I
•thorny	really know their story if I don't watch the plant all the way
Time from flower to seed	along. So I know every plant in the field. I know them
Seed dispersal mechanisms	intimately, and I find it a great pleasure to know them. {A
Runners—# per plant	scientist must have a feeling for the organism
SENESCENCE	Barbara McClintock, Nobel Prize winning geneticist.

| When do leaves wilt and die Do any parts remain alive through winter or drought? What do plants look like in winter or drought? | |

"Beginning Journal Pages

BUILDING LIFE STAGE OBSERVATIONS

THINGS TO LOOK FOR BELOW GROUND	

ROOTS
Shape
    •net-like
    •bunched
    *taproot
    •combination
 	
**UNDERGROUND FOOD
   STORAGE**
    •Tubers
    •Bulbs
    •Corms
    •Rhizomes
 	
**UNDERGROUND ASEXUAL
REPRODUCTION**
    •rhizomes
    •bulbs
    •corms
 	
OTHER
    •nodules
    ªgalls
 	
To observe some underground parts without digging up a whole plant, plant seed in potting soil around the edges of a clear plastic glass, water and observe roots as they grow.
	The indescribable innocence and benificense of Nature—of sun and wind and rain, of summer and winter—such health, such cheer, they afford forever!...Shall I not have intelligence with the Earth? Am I not partly leaves and vegetable mould myself?
	
	      Henry David Thoreau

"Beginning Journal Pages

KEEPING BLOOM CALENDARS

THINGS TO LOOK FOR	JAN FEB MARCH APRIL MAY JUNE JULY AUG SEPT OCT NOV DEC

Red Trillium

Deptford Pink

Coltsfoot

New England Aster

Be alert for the first blossoms of a given species to appear in your area. Guidebooks give a usual range for bloom time but actually the time varies from year to year in different locations

When do about 25% or the plants in a stand show blossoms?

When do about 50% of the plants show blooms/

When have almost all the plants in the stand show they have blossomed? Note that some will have already stopped blossoming.

When have almost all the blossoms withered and seeds have begun to show?

If it is true that the sun, the seasons, the waters, and human life itself go in cycles, the inference is that "there is time for all things," something different to be done at each stage of the cycle...Only when we realize that nothing Is new can we live with an intensity in which everything becomes new.

Northrop Frye, literary critic

"Beginning Journal Pages

VISITORS AND DISEASES

THINGS TO LOOK FOR	
What groups of insects visit the plant?	
How much time does each visitor spend on the plant?	
What do the various insects do to or with the plant?	
What other animals visit the plant and for what purpose?	
If ther is damage from a visitor does it endanger the entire plant?	The mutualistic connections between many plants and animals created by pollination systems are important in binding the machinery of nature into a fractional whole.

What signs do you see of plant diseases?
  •colored spots
  •odd growths
  •rusts
  •molds
	Paul Ehrlich, ecologist

Do these diseases seem to be life threatening to the plant or just a nuisance?	

"Beginning Journal Pages

GEMINATION EXPLORATIONS
OR
IT ISN'T EASY BEING GREEN

THINGS TO DO AND OBSERVE	
Mark off with string a square foot or yard	
Map all the seeds you can see on the ground inside that swuare(acorns, maple keys, or others)	
Count all the seed and record the number	
Return every few days and look at the seeds.	
How many seeds disappear between visits?	
What do you think happened to them? What clues do you have?	It is the story of all life that is holy and is good to tell, and of us two–leggeds sharing it with the four–leggeds and the wings of the air and all green things; for these are children of one mother and their father is one Spirit.
How long before some of the seeds begin to sprout and develop seed leaves?	
What % of the total original seeds germinate?	Black Elk, Sioux elder
How many of these survive to grow true leaves? What happened to the rest?	
What % of the original number of seeds survive to adolescence or beyond?	

KEEPING TRACK OF ASSOCIATES

THINGS TO LOOK FOR	
What other plant species are growing in the same area as the species you are focusing on?	

Where other specimens of your focus plant are growing, which of the plants observed above are
    •always present
    •occasionally present
    •seldom present	

Do you wee any signs that some of these other plants directly affect the growth of your focus plants?	

What factors seem to affect all the plants that are always present?
    •soil type
    •moisture level
    •access to sunlight	

Do your focus plants seem to give off chemical substance that discourage other species from growing too close to your focus species?	One exercises justice or injustice to plants and animals as well...Plants and animals also have a right to unfolding and self-realization. They have the right to live. Arne Naess, environmental philosopher

"Beginning Journal Pages

REVEALING TREE LIVES

THINGS TO LOOK FOR	
When do leaf buds open?	
When are next year's leaf buds formed?	
When does the tree flower?	
Approximately how old is the tree before it gets its first flowers?	
Which opens first leaves or flowers?	
When leaves fall, what do the leaf scars left behind look like?	
About how old is a trunk or branch before the smooth bark begins to crack an thicken?	
Is the pattern of cracking distinct for the trees you are studying?	
When do the first leaves begin to fall in autumn? From what sections of the tree?	
When have the majority of leaves fallen from the tree?	

What animal live in or on the tree?
    *nesting birds
    *squirrels
    *insects
    *spiders
    ?other	

Do young of the tree survive best in sun or shade?	
What mechanisms does the tree have for getting seeds to good places for them to germinate?	I am trying to save the knowledge that the forest and this planet are alive, to give it back to you who have lost the understanding..
Does the tree have deep or shallow roots?	Paiakan, contemporary Kayapo Indian leader
What other plants grow in the shade of the tree?	

"Beginning Journal Pages

Things to Look For	LIKIN' LICHENS

What is the basic growth form?
    crustose
    foliose
    fruiticose
 	
What type of substrate is it growing on?
    rock
    bark
    bare soil
 	
What is the general exposure of the plants to sunlight and prevailing winds?
 	
Can you determine rough growth rates for these plants?
 	
What reproductive structures cn you find?
    isidia
    soredia
    squamules	

	"Lichens belong to an endless suspensior in time out of which lives sense their moments of affinity, their opportunities to parasitize, to bond or devour. It is an awesome game hanging on eternities. The existence of a lichen depends on th centrifugal nature of all contrary forces or a scale that seems perilous to out short— term sense of things, thou exhilaration in the mind". John Hay

"Beginning Journal Pages

Things to look for	FERN FROLICS
What is the shape of the fern fronds?	
What is the shape of the individual pinnules on a frond?	
Are there separate fertile and sterile fronds?	

What is the pattern of the whole plant?
      clump
      circular
      linear	

Where on the pinnules do sori appear?	
What is the shape of the sori?	
What is the shape of the indusia?	
What do the croziers look like? Are they smooth or fuzzy?	
Can you locate any prothalia on the ground nearby?	
What animals are associated with these ferns?	
Do these plants move by growing at one end and dying off on the other?	
Are these plants growing in sunny dry ares or moist shady ones?	
Do these ferns seem to be competitors or stress-tolerators?	"There is more variation in the ferns than in probably any other comparable group of plants" Neil Jorgensen

"Beginning Journal Pages

Things to look for	Bountiful Bryophytes
You will need a handlens to observe most bryophytes	

What substrate is the moss growing upon?
    granite outcrop
    water-saturated soil
    rotting wood
    bare soil	

What is its growth pattern?
    mat
    mound
    thin carpet	

What exposure do the plants get?
    northern
    southern	

Are there fruiting bodies? Note time of year	
Examine the fruiting capsule. Carefully draw the calyptra opcrculum annulus peristome urn	
Find the rhizoids that hold the moss to its substrate. Is the attachment very firm? or rather loose?	What is it exactly that binds us so closely to living things? The biologist will tell you that life is the self-replication or giant molecules from lesser chemical fragments, resulting in the assembly of complex organic structures…The poet—in biologist will add that life is an exceedingly improbable state, metastable, open to other systems, thus ephemeral—and worth any price to keep. Edward O Wilson, entomologist and evolutionary biologist

"Beginning Journal Pages

THINGS TO DO AND LOOK FOR:	EXPLORING COMMUNITIES
Choose a habitat and establish measured study plots. List all the species found in each study plot. Determine the rough percentage of occupancy of each species. What species appear to be dominant? Are these species competitors, stress–tolerators, or ruderals? Note the seasonal growth patterns of the different species. Which species survive to sexual reproduction? Which species expand mainly by vegetative reproduction? Does the plant community in each plot appear stable or does it seem to be in transition? What are the different vertical zones in your plots?	
	"There are changes and re-associations going on in the soil and in the atmosphere, revolutions of a more reliable kind that move us to feelings we never knew we had. To have real rather than sentimental roots is to be in motion." John Hay

"Beginning Journal Pages

REFLECTIONS

THINGS TO THINK ABOUT

How has watching plants changed how I think about them?

How has watching plants changed how I think about myself?

How has watching plants changed how I view life?

What are things I like most about plants?

Do I think any differently know about mainting clipped laws or encouraging wild plants in my yard?

"Familiarity with things about one should not dull the edge of curiosity or interest. The walk you take today through woods and fields, or along the riverbank, is the walk you should take tomorrow, and next day, and next. What you miss once, you will hit upon next time. The happenings are at intervals and are irregular. The play of Nature has no fixed program. If she is not at home to-day, or is in a non committal mood, call tomorrow, or next week"
John Burroughs

8

A QUESTIONING FRAMEWORK FOR EXPLORING PLANT LIFE HISTORIES

Presented here is a list of questions relevant to each of the life history stages. The answers to these questions can provide the framework for a reasonably thorough life history study of a plant species. No one set of questions provides for all groups of plants, but these several sets are presented to cover a broad range. Questions such as these clearly are not complete, but they do establish a basic quest for knowledge about the lifeways of plants. If you get deeply involved in understanding how plants live, you will formulate a number of questions of your own to add to these lists.

FOR FLOWERING PLANT SPECIES
A.SEEDS

What do the seeds look like; what are their distinguishing features?

In what kind of structures are the seeds borne?

How many seeds per structure?

How big is the average seed?

What adaptations do the seeds have for dispersal?

What is the average time from flower fertilization to seed ripening?

Do the seeds sprout immediately or do they have a dormant period?

If the seeds have a period of dormancy, is the period determined genetically or environmentally?

What is the normal season for germination?

What are the enemies of the seeds?

What is the average distance the seeds are dispersed?

How long on average do the seeds appear to remain viable under field conditions?

B. SEEDLINGS (JUVENILE STAGE)

How does the embryo emerge from the seed? What structures grow first and fastest? What do the seedlings of the species look like; what are their distinguishing features? What temperature, moisture, and light conditions are needed for sprouting? How long after germination do the first true leaves appear?

Are young leaves significantly different in shape from mature ones? If yes, in what ways? How old is the seedling before it develops a fibrous or corky stem? Which develops more vigorously at first, root systems or leaves and stem? How long between germination and flowering?

C. MATURE PLANTS—FLOWERS

How long between formation of flower bud and the opening of that flower?

Do individual flowers remain open around the clock or do they open and close on a fairly fixed time schedule?

How long does an individual blossom last intact? What is the sequence in which various flower parts are lost?

What adaptations does the plant have for either self—or cross—pollination?

During what part of the bloom period does the flower produce odor or nectar, if it does at all?

What is the blooming period for the plant? For the species? In your locale? In its geographic rage? Is it a long—or short-day length bloomer or is it neutral?

What is the average number of blossoms per plant? Does this vary widely from year to year: If so, what factors influence the amount of bloom?

What factors injure the flower parts as the fertilized flower transforms into a fruit?

What is the sequence of opening of individual blossoms in a cluster?

D. MATURE PLANT—FRUIT

How long does it take for the ovary to develop from the flower into a fruit ripe for seed dispersal?

What is the method of seed release from the fruit?

What is the average number of seeds per fruit and fruits per plant?

What adaptations does the fruit have for dispersal?

E. MATURE PLANT VEGETATIVE REPRODUCTION

What structures of the plant are regularly used for vegetative reproduction?

What times of the year is vegetative reproduction most actively utilized?

Are different structure more heavily utilized at different times of the year?

What environmental condition favor vegetative reproduction over sexual reproduction?

F. MATURE PLANT—STEMS AND LEAVES

Is there a reasonably consistent number of leaves on any given stem at the time it ceases upward growth?

Is there a relationship between leaf size and shape and environmental conditions?

What factors seem most to affect rate of growth and/or premature cessation of growth?

What kinds of buds does the stem have? Where are they located?

What is the pattern of leaf arrangement on the stem (phyllotaxy)?

Are the stems primarily above, on, or below ground?

What are the enemies of the leaf? What is the average life span of an individual leaf?

G. MATURE PLANTS—ROOTS

How far down do the roots penetrate?

How far out from the stem do the roots spread?

Do the roots have corky bark? If yes, how extensive?

Do the roots enlarge for food storage?

What are the enemies of the roots?

Are there aerial or other adventitious roots?

Do the roots host mycorrhizal fungi?

H. GENERAL ITEMS

How long does an individual of the species live on average?

Hod does the species tolerate stress and/or disturbance?

With what species does it regularly associate? Does it have and obligate relationship with any of these?

What are its soil, moisture, light and temperature preferences?

What is the species appearance like at various key stages through the annual cycle?

What is the degree and nature of variability within the species?

How is the species adapted to (or co-evolved with) animal species?

What behavioral responses does it exhibit and to what stimuli?

APPENDIX A.

THE KEY TO
IDENTIFICATION

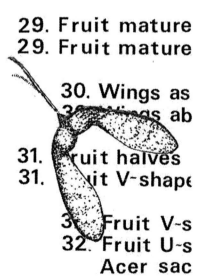

29. Fruit mature
29. Fruit mature

    30. Wings as
    3   s ab

31.   ruit halves
31.   it V-shape

   3 Fruit V-s
   32. Fruit U-s
     Acer sac

Your initial involvement with field botany may focus on developing a species inventory of an area of particular interest to you, or perhaps you will find significant enjoyment in getting to know the identity of as many different plant species as possible in whatever area of the globe you may find them. Whatever the motivation, tracking down the proper identification of any specimen involves close observation, development of skill in working through various identification "keys"—either visual or technical, and appreciation of the complexities of the plant world. It will also take you on a voyage into the esoteric language of botany

Over the past several centuries scientist have been closely examining the similarities and differences among the various living things on this planet. They have attempted to create systems of categories into which they can logically arrange the variety of life forms. As more and more information has accumulated and been evaluated, the various systems of classification have become increasingly sophisticated. But even the system we use today is only out present approximation of actual relationships and is constantly subject to fine-tuning. The rationale behind the current scientific classification, or *taxonomy*, of living things is the alleged evolutionary relationships among the various categories, or *taxa*, or life forms. As we add to our knowledge of each *taxon*, view often change about the degree of closeness or relationship to other taxa. In spite of our human desires to have neat, fixed sets of pigeon holes into which any given life form can be placed, nature refuses to cooperate fully and we are left with a certain amount of confusion. The taxonomy of plants is no different in this respect than classification of other life forms. All retain a certain amount of fluidity that seems to defy precision.

THE NOTION OF SPECIES

The basic unit of plant and animal classification is the species. At first glance it seems to be a clear enough concept. *By definition all members of a species should be able to interbreed and produce viable offspring that closely resemble their parents.* But examination of almost all species shows a range of variation that is open to interpretation as to whether or not it different enough to deserve separate identity as one species. Perhaps taxonomists should split the species into two or more or perhaps lump it along with another apparently closely related species.

Be aware of problems in identification and take them in stride as you attempt to hurdle them. Some variant specimens may be strikingly different in appearance from other members of the apparent species. Experiments in laboratories or test plots may show that variants interbreed normally with others of their apparent species even though they seldom get the chance in nature because of geographic isolation. In other cases, plants of a species may show individual variation as a response to local differences in the environment. Such genetic variants or ecological variants sometimes may be classified as subspecies or varieties. Some hybrids in the wild are the offspring of a cross between two distinct species. Some hybrids are fertile and produce vigorous second-generation offspring while others are partially or fully sterile. Hybrids show characteristics of both original parent species but not the entire characteristic of either parent. All such variations present problems in trying to make a firm determination of species affiliation of some specimens. Because of different reproduction strategies, some plant groups are more susceptible to confusing variations the are others, For instance, beware of sedges, hawthorns, and hawkweeds.

It is not my intent to confuse or discourage you with this discussion, but rather to help you understand that it is quite reasonable to expect that any given plants you may be trying to identify to species may not fit neatly into one of the preconceived species boxes presented by any of the identification tools we will soon be discussing. Even the so-called experts do not agree on just what constitute the boundaries of various taxa or how many species the known variations in a group represent. Some classifiers, taxonomists, re considered lumpers—that is, they lump together plants with several "minor difference" into one species. Others are splitters. They give greater weight to those "minor difference" and therefore describe two or more species in the same population. In Taxonomy of Flowering Plants, Taxonomist C.L. Porter sums it up in slightly more technical language thusly: "It must be apparent that no universal definition of species is likely to be forthcoming even though a definite concept may be formulated for any group of plants. When plants reproduce by purely sexual means, in the usual fashion, the problem is more easily resolved on the basis of sterility barriers and overall morphology and geography. But when plants reproduce asexually, by apomixis or other means, only experience and judgement can bring about a reasonable working system of classification. Perhaps it is reasonable, for practical purposes, to interpret a species as a recognizable and self-perpetuating population that is more or less isolated genetically as well as by its geographic distribution and environment."

While doing field studies, we do not have to be overly concerned about such professional taxonomic differences except to recognize that they do exist and that our best attempts to come up with positive species identification may be thwarted. It is usually possible to key a specimen to its larger categories of family and genus without identifying it to species. Initially is enough if you carefully prepare a voucher specimen of the plant under study so that a later date you and the botanical experts can focus on a more precise determination to species.

VISUAL KEYS FOR IDENTIFICATION

Over the past half-century botanists and naturalists have devised popular guides to the identification of the more common or conspicuous plant species. These guides tend to recognize an average person's aversion to working his or her way through most technical botanical keys or sorting through the specimens in an herbarium to match a labeled specimen with the unknown one in order to identify it.

In presenting his visual approach to wildflower identification, Roger Tory Peterson, an artist-naturalist, wrote: "Some people, those with orderly minds, are able to use technical keys in running down their flowers but many throw up their hands in despair because of the bewildering terminology...However, if one can master them, keys are the proper formal approach to flower identification. But, I am afraid, most of us belong to the picture-matching school, and it is for this audience that our Field Guide has been planned"

Today, most people who want to learn to identify wild plants begin with one or more of such visually oriented guides. All of them depend fundamentally on such visual cues as color, shape, and discriminating details of form. Ornithologist and naturalist Roger Tory Peterson developed an approach based on carefully delineated line drawings and paintings enhanced with arrows pointing to the most discriminating diagnostic features. Other authors in the field guide series he edited have used his system. These books provide assistance for identification primarily through matching specimens to pictures. Over all this series includes more species than any other does.

A number of field guides have been developed that use color photographs rather than drawings. At first these guides were not very satisfactory because reproduction of color photographs was relatively expensive, and to save money, most guides clustered many species on a page with such small photos that identification was difficult. In recent years the cost of reproduction of color photography has improved in cost and quality and now more guides have been produced so that the photos are of larger size.

These visually oriented identification guides have strengths and weaknesses that should be borne in mind by those planning to use them. Their biggest plus is relative ease of use because they depend largely on visual comparison for the first cut at eliminating species unlike the one you wish to identify. As Peterson said, it's mostly picture matching and you do not need to be aware of the subtle shades of meaning of hundreds of botanical terms.

Most of these guides arrange the species according to the color of their flowers, which is often their most obvious characteristic. But there can be confusion in some species. White trillium blossoms, for instance, change from white to deep pink as they age. You would tend to lookup and older bloom in the red category and you usually would not find it there. You would have to know by other criteria that although the specimen's dolor was different from others growing nearby, it was not a different species. Similarly, you may find an orchid that looks like pink lady-slipper (Cypripedium acaule) but it has a pure white flower. If you look it up in the section on white blossoms, you probably would not find it, because it is a genetic variety (Cypripedium acaule var. alba) There are any number of examples of this sort that could be cited but these give some indication of the weakness of this color-based system of sorting out species.

Among the visual guides, the illustrations vary in their accuracy and methods of presenting the most diagnostic features of a species. Photographs despite their realism illustrate only one example of a species. Given the variability within any particular species, your unknown specimen may look very much like the guide's photo or it may appear disturbingly different yet still be that species in the photo. Drawings can share this same weakness, but the artist can alter things to present more of the variations of the species within one drawing and also can carefully change leaf position or make other perspective changes that will better illustrate a diagnostic feature. Thus, many people still feel that, unless photos have been exceeding carefully selected, an artist's renderings are more useful than photos in identification. There are, of course, some things that are usually more effectively presented by photos than drawings, such as tree bark. Each approach has its advantages and drawbacks.

I find that no one system or series is satisfactory by itself. Normally I use several different field guides in a making a determination, crosschecking one against another. For one thing, there is not visual guide to all the plant species of a region, and different authors make different determination about which species they will include in their guide. One field guide to a geographic region may include my unknown specimen while it is absent from another guide to the same region. It seems to be one of the infamous Murphy's Laws that I always look in the latter first!

Visual guides use clues to identification that are not necessarily based on the anatomical features that plant taxonomists use to determine the evolutionary relationships of species. Such keys are termed artificial keys as opposed to the natural keys of technical literature. A major concern of many botanists is that people who learn to identify plants by using the artificial keys are not apt to come away with any basic understanding of the fundamental characteristics of the major plant families. To the beginner at plant identification this may seem unimportant, but as you become more deeply involved you will find yourself wanting to identify plants not included in the usual field guides. It is then that the knowledge of plant family characteristics begins to emerge as a distinct handicap that results in spending inordinately more time than necessary in trying to use the technical keys. Among the visual keys, Peterson's wildflower guide uses a symbolic set of clues to the plant families—based on the key characteristics of the families—to help those who desire to gain some basic knowledge of the family characteristics and the genera and species that share them.

A BRIEF GUIDE TO SOME USEFUL VISUAL KEYS

The Peterson Field Guide Series from Houghton-Mifflin including:

A Field Guide to Wildflowers of Northeastern and Central North America
A Field Guide to Pacific States Wildflowers
A Field Guide to Edible Wild Plants of Northeastern and Central N.A.
A Field Guide to Rocky Mountain Wildflowers
A Field Guide to Ferns and their Related Families
A Field Guide to Trees and Shrubs
Grasses: An Identification Guide

The National Audubon Society Field Guide Series from Knopf including:

North American Wildflowers—Eastern Region
North American Wildflowers—Western Region
Field Guide to Trees—Eastern Region

The Golden Field Guide Series from Golden Press including:

Trees
Wildflowers of North America

Golden Guides from Golden Press including:

Trees
Wildflowers
Weeds

Also:

Dwelley, Marilyn
Trees and Shrubs of New England 2nd ed.
2000
Camden, Maine: Down East Books

Brode, Irwin B. and Stephen Sharnoff
Lichens of North America
2001
New Haven, Conn.: Yale University Press

In addition many national parks sell local guides to plants that are basically visual and focus on the flora of that immediate region

ON TO TECHNICAL KEYS

Why is it so important to become familiar with the family characteristics? Sooner or later you will have to turn to technical keys to identify some pant or plants that have stimulated your curiosity. Most of these are in thick tome that include several thousand species usually arranged according to the approved botanical order. The hierarchy of arrangements is as follows. Phylum

Class

Order

Family

Genus

Species

The first three taxa are large categories helpful as a quick start in deciding what part of a kingdom you to-be-identified specimen belongs to.

The family level of the hierarchy is the taxon where the next very important cut can be made to narrow down the choices. You still then go on to determine the proper genus within the family in t o search further among the various species descriptions to find the one that matches your unknown specimen. Coming to terms with the use of technical keys involves two basic skills, mastering the puzzle-solving structure of a key's format and mastering botanical terminology. Both involve a certain mind set, concentration and determination.

Although most people today begin with the popular picture-matching guides, there are a few popular field identification guides and simple keys that allow for a reasonable transition to the highly technical keys of such classic reference as *Gray's Manual of Botany, 8th edition* and *Britton and Brown's Illustrated Flora*

WORKING A TECHNICAL KEY

The basic concept of a technical (natural) identification key is quite simple. You are given a set of descriptive choices, or leads, in the form of phrases or sentences. Normally there are two such choices forming a couplet. A dichotomous key is composed of such couplets but in other kinds of keys there may be more leads. Each lead of the couplet is given the same number and a letter designation. You make an appropriate choice from the leads and follow the line to the right, where you will either find a number that represents the next set of choices you should pursue or the name of the taxon you have been seeking. If the latter, you have completed your quest. The number of choices you will have to pursue before reaching a final determination is highly variable.

Another common variation of key form frequently used by botanists has and indented format; each successive set of choices is indented further from the left martin of the page, thus obviating the need for numbers and letters. Formats that vary significantly from these two formats are usually explained in users' note at the beginning of the key.

Observe the following common-sense rules in working specimens through a key:

1. Read through each of the choices or leads very carefully, even if the first statement appears to be the appropriate one. You may find that another lead is even more descriptive of your specimen.

2. If measurements are given in the key, actually measure your specimen. Don't guess.

3. Where technical botanical terms are given, look up the exact meaning of the term if you are at all uncertain about it. Again, don't guess.

4. Don't base conclusion on an inadequate portion of a specimen. Even on a single plant there will be a certain degree of variability, so if possible use observations of several specimens of the same type to arrive at your determination of species. Another of Murphy's Laws is that given random choice a beginner tends to choose the most atypical part of a specimen upon which to base determinations!

5. Key makers are, after all, only human, so sometimes choices clear to them are much less clear to others. When you come to an unclear set of choices follow each lead to see if the information of one of them perhaps relates to your specimen.

Some people get a great deal of pleasure from working specimens through the various choices of a technical key to arrive at a final determination of species. There is the same kind of challenge as solving a mystery story or finding the solution to a puzzle. Keying often has the added challenge and frustration of running a maze, for there may be blind alleys that lead nowhere or to a false conclusion.

Errors may occur because of imperfect construction of the key itself, but more frequently it is because of pitfalls inherent in unfamiliarity with botanical terminology and failure to follow common-sense rule 3 above. The potential for confusion is highlighted by Roger T Peterson's note that "There are at least 60 ways of saying that a plant is not smooth. They range from aculeate, asperous, and bristly to villous, viscid, and wooly" Each has a very technical meaning to the botanist and represents a broad range of subtle differences. Despite the implications of their supposed exactitude of meaning, not all botanists use the same term for the same given shade of variation in a plant's structure. Thus, you may have a slightly different impression of a character mentioned in a key that did the person who prepared it. This may well lead you down dead ends and byways in a key which, depending upon your personality, are guaranteed to heighten either your fun or your frustration. Technical keys seem most enjoyable to people with orderly minds and a capacity for using words in a precise and narrowly defined manner. For others technical keys remain an all-but-inescapable necessary evil. SOME USEFUL TECHNICAL KEYS

Classics include *Gray's Manual of Botany, 8ᵗʰ edition* and *Britton and Brown's Illustrated Flora*

Newcomb's Wildflower Guide, Lawrence Newcomb, Boston: Little Brown

Weeds of the Northeast by Richard Uva, Cornell University Press Mosses with a Hand Lens by A.J. Grout and Mary Thayer, author published, Newfane Vermont

Agnes Chase's First Book of Grasses by Clark and Pohl, Washington, DC: Smithsonian Books.

How to Identify Grasses and Grass-like Plants by H.D. Harrington

Field Guide to the Grasses, Sedges, and Rushes of the Northern United States By Edward Knobel

How to Know the Mosses and Liverworts by Conard, Redfearn, Cawley and Jaques, McGraw-Hill

Lichen Handbook by Mason Hale, Washington, DC: Smithsonian Books

How to Know the Plant Families by Jaques

FACING THE LANGUAGE OF BOTANY

In a modern, living language, words tend to go through historical changes in use and meaning. What may begin as street slang may end up in broad common usage. For example grass once meant those plants of lawn, hayfields and high plains; today it is commonly used to refer to the distinctly un-grass-like marijuana and to "bluegrass" music. Such shifts in meaning in a living language make any commonly agreed upon, precise meaning for words to some degree ephemeral. If such precision possible, there would be little need to update our standard dictionaries periodically.

On the other hand science has a strongly felt need for stable, precise meanings for words. To achieve stability, a so-called "dead" language, Latin (augmented with classical Greek), is utilized. Since no modern peoples speak Latin today as a daily language, the meanings of its words and word endings remain reasonably fixed and thus more precise. Actually, the language is not truly dead, for it is modified by the construction of new words by the Vatican and scientists who may "latinize" words to use in scientific names to keep it up-to-date with new discoveries and inventions. This use of Latin meets the needs of professional scientist reasonably well but tend to frustrate the amateur who fins him-or herself learning new subject matter by means of a new and strange language.

However, scientific names and technical terms are understood by scientifically-oriented people of many different languages. Whether the people of a nation know the common yellow-flowered, dooryard plant as a dandelion, dent de lion, or los dientes del lion, their botanists will know it as a member of the genus *Taraxacum,* and most likely as *Taraxacum officinale.* Each species has its binomial name composed of a Latin noun to designate the genus plus a Latin adjective to designate the species. Many people are most frustrated when they face a scientific name because they are baffled by how to pronounce it. They see each term as a potential tongue-tripping embarrassment, throw up their hands, and give up. It is seldom realized how many technical names are now in everyday usage—for example, chrysanthemum, gladiola, clintonia, trillium, nasturtium, and spirea. Other differ only slightly from the Latin term—violet *(Viola),* lupine *(Lupinus), rose* (Rosa).

If you are exploring the plant world on your own, taking the effort to cope with botanical language may seem like a lot of work for nothing. But if you start fraternizing with serious amateur or professional botanists, read in botany books, or try to key out uncommon species in the technical keys you will soon find yourself lost if lacking some familiarity with the botanical language.

I still recall vividly may first awakening to this fact. As a college undergraduate with primarily a zoological background, I set forth one bracing fall day with one of my biology professors and h is botanical friend on a canoe trip into a local wild area to survey it as a possible acquisition by the Nature Conservancy. Before long I felt as though I had set forth with a couple of Chinese for all of their conversation that I could understand. I knew the common names of the trees, shrubs, and wildflowers we were drifting past, but they communicated only in a rapid-fire string of scientific names that were hastily scribbled down in a notebook. I knew almost none of these scientific names but was embarrassed to admit it, so I spent most of the trip in silence and ignorance, forced to be content absorbing the pervading beauty of the place. I vowed that I would never let myself get caught in such a situation again.

The next day I set about listing all the native trees and shrubs on campus or at least those that I passed on my various daily routes. I then wrote down each plant's scientific name and began memorizing. Each day as I walked to and from class I would greet each species by its proper name—"Good morning *Thuja canadesis";* Good morning. *Ulmus americana;* Good morning. *Lyriodendron tulipifera,"* and so forth. Soon these names flowed as easily from my tongue as everyday English, and adding scientific names to my vocabulary came much easier as I learned new species.

Approach botanical lingo as you would any other new language. Discover which are the most basic terms for whatever group you are working with and memorize them You may even want to go so far as to make up vocabulary cards with the term on one side and its meaning on the other. In spare moments you can work through these "flash cards" to reinforce you memory of the terms. As you master the basics, you will add some of the less common terms to you collection of flash cards and eventually to your mental repertoire. It generally takes much less time than you originally expected before the once strange and frightening language of botany begins to look more familiar and friendly. Like many new ventures, mastering the language of botany is best accomplished by taking one step, and one day, at a time a patiently refusing to be cowed by the strange and unfamiliar. Ultimately it is cracking a secret code that opens new avenues of excitement and happiness.

Most technical keys have a glossary that you can use to determine the meaning of particular words. The following tool may help you decipher the subtleties of some of the terms:

Plant Identification Terminology: An Illustrated Glossary 2nd edition by James G and Melinda Wolf Harris from Spring Lake Publications

NATIVE PLANT SOCIETIES

Originally compiled by the North American Native Plant Society and updated by Jack Sanders.

STATE AND PROVINCIAL NATIVE PLANT SOCIETIES

ALABAMA
Alabama Wildflower Society 11120 Ben Clements Road Northport, AL 35475

ALASKA
Alaska Native Plant Society P,O, Boxl41613 Anchorage, AK 99514-1613

ALBERTA
Alberta Native Plant Council 52099, Garneau Postal Outlet Edmonton, AB, Canada T6G2T5 www.anpc.ab.ca

ARIZONA
Arizona Native Plant Society P.O. Box 41206, Sun Station Tucson, AZ 85717-1206 AZNPS.org

ARKANSAS
Arkansas Native Plant Society P.P. Box 250250 Little Rock, AR 72225

BRITISH COLUMBIA
Garry Oak Meadow Preservation Society A-954 Queens Avenue Victoria, BC, Canada V8T1M6

Native Plant Society of British Columbia 2012 William Street Vancouver, BC V5:2X6 www.npsbc.org inform,ation@npsbc.org

Victoria Horticultural Society Native Plant Study Group P.O. Box 5081, Ppostal Stn B Victoria, BB, Canada V8R6N3

CALIFORNIA
California Native Plant Society 1722Jst. Suite 17 Sacremento, CA 95814-2931

COLORADO
Colorado Native Plant Society P.O. Box 200, Fort Collins CO 80522-0200

CONNECTICUT
Connecticut Botanical Society P.O. Box 9004 New Haven, CT 06532-0004 Ct-botanical-societty.org

DELAWARE
Delaware Native Plant Society P.O. Box 369 Dover, DE 19903

www.delawarewnativeplants.org
dnps@delawarenativeplants.org

Mount Cuba Center for the Study of
Native Piedmont Flora Box3570,
Greeneville, DE 19807

DISTRICT OF COLUMBIA
Botanical Society of Washing ton
Dept. of Botany, NHB 166 Smith-
soonian Institution, Washingtyon,
D.C. 230560

FLORIDA
Florida Native Plant Society
P.O. Box 690278
Vero Beach FL 32969-0278
www.fnps.org

GEORGIA
Georgia Native Plant Society P.O.
Box 422085 Atlanta, GA 30342-
2085
www.gnps.org/
Phone 770-343-6000
E-mail: GLNPs@Mindspring.com

IDAHO
Idaho Native Plant Society P.O. Box
9451 Boise, ID 83707-3451

ILLINOIS
Illinois Native Plant Society Forest
Glen Preserve 20301 E.900 North
Road Westville IL 61883
www.il-onps.org

INDIANA
Indiana Native Plant and Wildflower
Society
16508 Oak Road
Westfield IN 46074-9436

IOWA
Iowa Native Plant Society Depart-
ment of Botany 341A Bessey Hall
Iowa State University Ames, I
50011+1020
E-mail:dlewis@iastate.e3du

KANSAS
Kansas Wildflower Society
R.L. McGregor Herbarium,
University of Kansas
2045 Constant Avenue
Lawrence, KA 66047-3729
www.cs.hcsston.edu/kws

KENTUCKY
Dept of Biological Science E. Kentucky University Richmond, KY
40475

LOUSIANA
Louisiana Native Plant Society 216
Caroline Dorman Road Saline, LA
71070
www.lnps.org

MAINE
Josselyn Botanical Society 566 N.
Auburn Road Auburn, ME 04210

MARYLAND
Maryland Native Plant Society

P.O. Box 4877
Silver Springs, MD 20914
www.mdflora.org

MASSACHUSETTS
New England Wild Flower Society
180 Hemenway Road Framingham,
MA 01701-2699 www.newfs.org

MICHIGAN
Michigan Botanical Club 7951 Walnut Avenuje Newaygo, MI 49337
www.michbotclub.org

MINNESOTA
Minnesota Native Plant Society
220 Bio. Sci. Center
University of Minnesota144 Gortner
Avenue
St. Paul MN 55108-1020
www.stolaf.edu/dcpts/biology/mnps

MISSISSIPPI
Mississippi Native Plant Society
Attn: Bob Brzuszek, LCrosby Arboretum P.O. Box 190 Picayune, MS
29466

MISSOURI
Missouri Native Plant Society
P.O. Box 20073
St. Louis, MO 63144-0073
www.missouri.edu/~umoherb/monps

MONTANA
Montana Native Plant Society P.O.
Box 8783 Missoula,. MT 59807-8782

NEVADA
Northern Nevada Native Plant Society
Box 8965
Reno, NV 89507+8965

NEW JERSEY
The Native Plant Society of New Jersey
Office of Continuing Professional
Education
Cook College
102 Ryders Lane
New Brunswick, NJ 08901+8519
www.npsnj.org

NEWFOUNDLAND
The Wildflower Society of
Newfoundland/Labrador
c/o Botanical Garden, Memorial
University
St. Johns, NF, Canada A1C5S7
www.chem.mun.ca/~.hclase/wf/
index.ht
ml

NEW MEXICO
Native Plant Society of new Mexico
P.O. Box 5917 Santa Fe,NM 87502

NEW YORK
New York Flora Association New
York State Museum 3132 CEC
Albany, NY 12230

The Finger Lakes Native Plant Society

Of Ithaca
532 Cayuga Heights Rd.
Ithaca, NY 14850

Niagra Frontier Botanical Society
Buffalo Museum of Science 1020
Humboldt Parkway Buffalo, NY
14211

NORTH CAROLINA
North Carolina Native Plant Society
North Carollina Botanical Garden
Totten Garden Center 3375
Univ. of North Carolina
Chapel Hill, NC 27599-3375
www.ncwildflower.org

Yellow Creek Botanical Institure
P.O. Box 1751 Robbinsville, NC
28771

NOVA SCOTIA
Nova Scotia Wild Flora Society
Nova
Scotia Museum
1747 Summer Street
Halifax, NS, Canada B3H3A6

OHIO
Cincinnati Wild Flower Preservation
Society
9005 Decima Street
Cinncinnati, OH 45242

Native Plant Society of Northeastern
Ohio
640 Cherry Park Oval
Aurora, OH 44203

Communities.msn.com/NativePlant
SocietyofNortheast Ohio

Ohio Native Plant Society 6 Louise
Drive Chagrin Falls, OH 44022

ONTARIO
Canadian Wildflower Society, East
Toronto
43 Anaconda Avenue
Scarbourough, ON Canada
M1L4M1

Canadian Wildflower Society, Dog-
tooth—Wellington Botany Dept.,
University of Guelph Guelph, ON
Canada N1G2W1

Canadian Wildflower Society-Lon-
don 1 Windsor Crescent London,
ON Canada N6C1V6

Field Botanists of Ontario
c/o W.D. McIlveen
RR#1 Acton, ON Canada L7J2L7
www.trentuxa?frbo/

OKLAHOMA
Oklahoma Native Plant Society
Tulsa Garden Center 2435 S. Peoria
Tulsa, OK 74114-1350

OREGON
Native Plant Society of Oregon P.O.
Box 902 Eugene, OR 97440
www.NPOregon.org

PENNSYLVANIA
Botanical Society of Western
Pennsylvania
5837 Nicholson Street
Pittsburg, PA 15217

Delaware Valley Fern/Wildflower
Society
P.O. Box 281
State College, PA 16804-0281
www.pawildflower.org

QUEBEC
FloraQuebecca
445 rue du Portage
Mont-Laurier, Quebec, Canada,
J9L2A1
www.floraquebecca.qc.ca

RHODE ISLAND
Rhode Island Wild Plant Society
P>)>Box 114
Peace Dale, RLI 02883-0114

SOUTHEAST
Southern Appalachian Botanical
Society Newberry College 2100 College Street Newberry, SC 29108

SOUTH CAROLINA
South Carolina Native Plant Society
Box 759 Pickens, SC 29671
www.scnps.org

SOUTH DAKOTA
Great Plains Native Plant Society
P.O.Box 461, Hot Springs, Sd 57747
info@gpnps.org

TENNESSEE
Tennessee Native Plant Society
c/o Department of Botany, University of Tennessee Knoxville, TN
37996-1100

The Wildflower Society Goldsmith
Civic Garden Center 750 Cherry
Road Memphis, TN 38119-4699

TEXAS
Native Plant Society of Texas
P.O. Box 891
Georgetown, TX 7862790891
www.npsot.org

UTAH
Utah Native Plant Society
P.O.Box 520041
Salt Lake Cit, UT 84152-0041
www.xmission.com/~unps/
index.html

VIRGINIA
Virginia Native Plant Society 400
Blandy Farm Lane #2 Boyce, VA
22620 www.vnps.org

WASHINGTON
Washington Native Plant Society
7400 Sand Point Way NE Seattle,
WA 98115
www.wnps.org

WEST VIRGINIA
West Virginia Native Plant Society

P.O. Box, New Haven, WV 25265-0808

WISCONSIN
Botanical Club of Wisconsin
Wisconsin Academy of Arts, Sciences an Letters 1922 University Ave. Madison, WI
53705

WYOMING
Wyoming Native Plant Society 1604 Grand Ave., Suite 2 Laramie, WY 82070

ADDITIONAL RELEVANT PLANT ORGANIZATIONS IN NORTH AMERICA

American Association of Field Botanists
P.O. Box 23542
Chattanooga TN 374Native Plant Society22

Center for Plant Conservation Missouri Botanical Garden P.O. Box 299 St. Louis, MO 63166

North American Native Plant Society Box 84, Postal Station D Etobicoke, ON Canada M9A4X1

APPENDIX D—THE PLANT OBSERVERS' TOOLKIT AND QUADRATS AND TRANSECTS

A hallmark of the human species is our capacity for making and using tools to compensate for the limitations of our anatomy or mental capacity. Field botany from its inception has relied less on a complex tool kit than a great man other human activities, but it certainly does have its basic tools. The more deeply involved you become in the why and wherefore of plant activities, the more you have to rely on sensory—extending tools.

In the sections that follow, we will discuss some of the criteria to consider in choosing commercially available equipment and also indicate a few reliable sources for those specialized items not widely available. Much more equipment is discussed here than is needed on a regular basis; much is appropriate only to certain special studies.

Despite elaboration on equipment here, remember that considerable fun and enlightenment can achieved with only the perceptual equipment you were born with and a notebook and pencil to record your observations. A good hand lens and a camera also greatly enrich your general ability to observe and record. Beyond these few items, you need for any other equipment depends upon your degree of involvement in specific types of study. Never let the tools of the trade obscure the purpose of your exploration; tools should always remain means rather than ends in themselves.

OBSERVATIONAL AIDS

Magnifiers. Among the most rewarding tools of the field botanist is a hand magnifying glass. It reveals enlarge details of plant structures that are ordinarily missed by the unaided eye, such as the architecture of flower parts, location of nectaries, various textures of a leaf's surface and much more. A diversity of magnifiers is available, but some types are more suitable for fieldwork than others.

The big round "Sherlock Holmes" magnifiers are available in many local stores. While good aids for reading for some people, the are not particularly useful for plant watchers. They do have a large field of view, but they usually have a magnification too small to be very useful in plant observation. With most reading magnifiers, magnification is only around one—and-one half to two times actual size, but for most botanical viewing magnification from 5x to 10x is most useful.

The larger the magnification the smaller the field of view you have and to achieve sharp focus, the closer the magnifier must be to the object being viewed. Thus, greater magnification creates a tradeoff problem of getting adequate light on the subject. The chart below gives a close approximation of the working distance (distance between object and lens when in focus) available for a variety of magnifications.

MAGNIFICATION (X)	WORKING DISTANCE (in)
1.75	14
2.25	8
2.75	6
2.76	3
3	3.5
5	2

7	1.5
10	1.
14	.75
20	.5

To use a magnifier, put it to your eye and maneuver the object to be viewed to the proper distance from the magnifier Some magnifiers are designed with a clear plastic base that lets in light while spacing the object correctly from the lens for proper focus. With such magnifiers the instrument is either paced on the object or the object is brought to rest on the magnifier base.

Some excellent and relatively inexpensive hand lenses have been designed for elementary school science activities. The best or these can be nested together to increase magnification. The lenses are plastic, however, and scratch easily. When in the field I carry one around my neck on a lanyard and use it more often than my better lenses. Glass lenses are more durable and more expensive. Among botanical hand lenses, the best is considered to be the Hastings magnifier, a highly corrected, triplet lens. Judge almost as good is the optically corrected, single-lens Coddington magnifier. Many people prefer a magnifier with three foldout lenses for differing magnification. Each lens can be used singly or can be combined for greater magnification. Only you can determine which type or brand is best for your needs and pocketbook.

Pocket Microscopes. For most fieldwork, magnifiers are quite adequate, but some people are interested in examining stomata of leaves and other very small plant structures. For them, one of the pocket microscopes may be a useful field tool. Most of these instruments are four or five inches long and range in magnification from 20x to 50x, with 50x being the most common. Because they must be brought within less than half an inch of the object to achieve focus, adequate light in the field is often a problem. The field of view of most of these scopes is only about two millimeters. Some of the instruments have optical reticules calibrated for accurate measurement of objects under the scope.

Standard Microscopes. A high quality microscope costs several hundred dollars and is not a profitable investment for the amateur unless you plan to use it frequently. To meet most needs for a microscope you are best advised to establish a relationship with a local high school or college biology teacher who will permit you occasional access to the school's microscopes.

For most botany work a stereomicroscope is usually far more useful than a monocular microscope.

BOTANICAL COLLECTING EQUIPMENT

Vasculum. When collecting specimens, voucher or others, you should keep them as fresh as possible until you can take time to prepare them properly for pressing and drying. A large, plastic self-sealing bag is generally suitable for keeping specimens moist and uncrushed. I always carry a few in my daypack just to be prepared. Carry a few paper towels as well, these to be moistened and put in the bag with the specimens. Leave air in the bag when you seal it to provide a cushion against accidental crushing.

People planning to do a lot of collecting may want to acquire a true botanical vasculum in which to carry their plants. A vasculum is usually a lightweight metal cylinder with a hinged door and catch. The whole device is carried over the shoulder y a strap. Usually each specimen is tagged and wrapped in moist toweling or newsprint before being put in the vasculum. Such a vasculum does provide good protection to the specimens, but it is an awkward, clumsy addition to the field gear. It is most valuable only to an avid, systematic collector.

Plant Press. A plant press is the key device in preparing, your voucher specimens. For casual use, an old city phone book may be used as a plant press, but if you plan to prepare any number of specimens it is worth it to purchase a good plant press made from high grade materials.

When selecting a commercially made plant press, remember that softwoods are more subject to bowing than are hardwoods. This will result in uneven pressure on the specimens. Hardwoods survive more hard usage in the field. Brass or copper rivets and fasteners are less likely to corrode or rust than other commonly used metals. Straps should be made of tightly woven cotton webbing with positive locking; lever-controlled spring buckles and have strap-ends with a metal protector to prevent fraying.

Plant Press Accessories. For occasional preparation of voucher specimens, pieces of corrugated cardboard box and newspapers, or desk blotters, will suffice as ventilators and absorbers, respectively. But if you plan to press plants regularly, it is worth investing in professional-grade-corrugated ventilators and dryers, for they have a higher rate of ventilation and absorption than most homemade equivalents. Between uses hang y our dryers on a clothesline in the sun to remove moisture and ready them for reuse. For best results, keep them stored in a dry place with a supply of moisture-absorbing crystals.

One item you should not scrimp on is your herbarium mounting paper. Most readily available papers in stationery stores are acid-based and become brittle and yellow with age. With such paper a specimen may well outlast the paper.

A good herbarium mounting paper is one with a high rag content that will remain flexible and not discolor with age. If you are preparing voucher specimens with the future in mind, assure that future by using high-grade paper and Archer adhesive

MEASURING AND TESTING EQUIPMENT

Choosing equipment for environmental measuring and testing first involves determining the degree of accuracy your investigations demand so that you can select instruments that deliver that degree of accuracy. The more accuracy required from an instrument, the greater its price as a rule. For example, a simple test kit for determining pH of soil sample cost only a few dollars but it will only indicate the broad pH category which may be generally sufficient for a gardener's purposes. But pH is calculated on a logarithmic scale, each numerical division representing ten times more or less hydrogen ions than the than adjacent number. When you need to know the pH level within each division, as you might if you are monitoring impact of acid rain on soils, you need a much more sensitive pH-measuring device. Such devices are likely to cost you hundreds of dollars more than the gardener's kits.

pH Testing. The most readily available pH testing materials are those from garden supply companies for testing garden soil and from pool supply companies for testing water. These materials are convenient but often limited in the pH range they cover. Test papers to test the full range of pH are available from most biological supply houses and are the most practical for moderately accurate measurements.

The pH meters with a dial and probes available in many garden supply stores are useful enough for crude calculations but, although they look more sophisticated than the color-matching chemical kits and papers, they are not more accurate and their probe-elements must be carefully cleaned after each use or they loose their effectiveness.

With all these simple testing devices—indeed, with all pH testing—you must be alert to the pH of any water you use to mix with the soil sample because its own pH contaminates the sample. Use distilled or bottled spring water that has a pH as close as possible to 7.

Soil Moisture Testing. Measuring soil moisture is difficult, but today there are many more sophisticated instruments available for doing this than there were only a few years ago. In most horticultural shops you can purchase two-pronged moisture meters to test the degree of dryness in you flowerpot soil. The instruments work in open fields and woods but not as well as in containers. They do not seem to be highly reliable although they are reasonably affordable. A better device available today is called an irrometer and it is in effect a "dummy root". It has a gauge attached to indicate the amount of tension a root must exert to get water. Irrometers come in a variety of lengths from 6" to 72" to test different root zones in the soil.

Chemical Testing Kits. Testing water and soil for minerals, nutrients, and other chemical is time-consuming and can become quite expensive if you do a number of tests of a variety of sites. There is virtually nothing you can do along this line with homemade materials; you must rely on the commercial kits and their refills.. Some kits are designed with an individual researcher in mind, others for classes of students. Scan the catalogs carefully and buy only what you need.

Light meters. To test the light intensity of an area, you can use standard photographic light meters, new independent light meters are getting scarcer and more expensive as modern cameras tend to come with light meters built in. For your work you will want a light meter that registers directly in foot-candles. Light meters fortunately last well and you may be able to pick up a good secondhand one at reasonable cost. Longtime photographers may have and unused one around the house that was retired when they bought new, up-to-date cameras.

Thermometers. Thermometers are among those measuring instruments where degree of desired accuracy is a particularly key factor in deciding how much of an investment to make. Another factor to consider is the degree of use they will receive; thermometers tend to break easily and if they are likely to get plenty of field use and abuse it's worth investing in more rugged models.

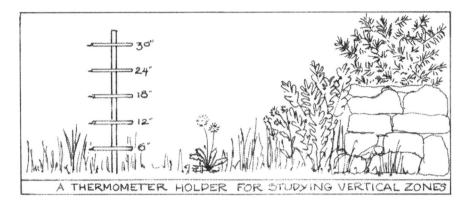

Figure D-1

Inexpensive models tend to be glass tubes clipped to a calibrated metal frame. These tubes can move slightly in the frames and thus give inaccurate readings. If you purchase several of these thermometers for cost reasons, you should lay them all out together along with a thermometer of proven accuracy. After the temperature readings have had a chance to stabilize, either shift individual tubes slightly so that all register the same reading as the master thermomet5er or add a taped note to each instrument indicating how many degrees plus or minus it varies from the standard so you can adjust any future readings of each to achieve a constancy among you instruments. With better thermometers, the glass tube itself is calibrated, thus reducing error.

Most thermometers are designed for use in air or water. If you want to take a soil reading, first poke a hole with a pencil or stick, then insert the thermometer; fewer thermometers get broken that way. Better still, purchase an armored soil thermometer designed for such work.

Make a protective case in which to carry you thermometers to reduce breakage and keep calibrations from wearing or chipping off. For general work, a thermometer that screws into a metal or plastic carrying case is a worthwhile investment.

Though expensive there are sophisticated thermometers that can probe very small spaces such as the surface of a flower or leaf. Such instruments use thermocouples to take the reading and are primarily wired to give a digital readout.

Soil Auger. When testing soil, you may want to examine the soil profile of take samples at various depths for chemical testing. The tool for this is a soil auger that is simply a large bore bit on a long handle that can be screwed into the soil and when lifted out will remove a core of it. They are commonly engineered to come apart at various points along the shank for convenient storage and handling and so that that the shank can receive extra length to go deeper. Also a special core tip can be attached that removes a solid soil pub from soils of appropriate consistency.

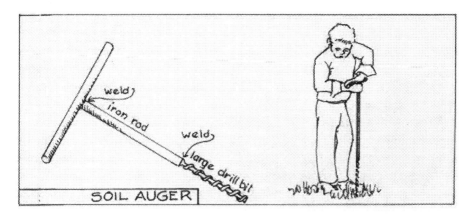

Figure D-2

Soil sieves. To determine the nature of aggregates in the soil and the amount of certain categories of particles, put soil samples through a set of soil sieves. Standard size mesh openings pre provided by commercially obtainable nesting sieves.

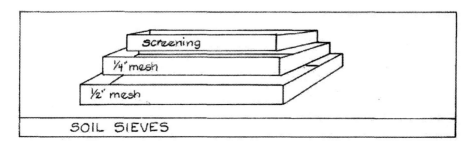

Figure D-3

Increment Borers. Increment borers are precision instruments that require good care in use and maintenance. They are readily available from forestry supply houses. They are very useful because the cores they remove reveal much about the history or a particular tree or woodland. They are well worth the investment if you enjoy discovering more about the history of particular trees or woodlands.

There are two major parts to the instrument: the borer and the extractor. The borer drilling into the tree to create the core; the extractor frees the core and removes it from the borer for examination. Borers come in a variety of lengths ranging in two-inch increments from 6" to20". The most common core diameters are .157", 169", and .200" It is easier to drill the smaller diameters since friction is less, but the resulting core is also a bit harder to remove, preserve, and read.

When you purchase an increment borer, two accessories are worth your consideration: a holster for ease of carrying and to help prevent loss in the field; and a sharpening kit, for a dull bit makes hard work in securing a core. Increment borers should be cleaned with a solvent after use because tree pitch and dried sap on cutting blades and tube increases friction making the instrument more frustrating to use.

Diameter Tape. Those people who keep track of tree size may want to carry a diameter tape with them in the field. Such tapes are available commercially, but you can make one simply enough by purchasing a roll of binding tape and marking off that tape at 31/2" intervals. Each such interval equals one inch of tree diameter, thus the tape will let you read the tree's diameter directly. Lacking a diameter tape, you can use a regular measuring tape to get the circumference in inches and then multiply that figure by. 318 to get the diameter. With today's pocket calculators, that is no real chore.

UNDERWATER GEAR

The world of underwater equipment continues to expand rapidly, so it would be foolish to try and give specific advice on selecting materials Comments here are limited to general things to be look for with particular reference to underwater botany needs.

Face mask. One of the more important pieces of equipment for underwater studies is the facemask. Choose one with maximum visibility, peripheral as well as straight ahead. Human faces vary extensively in shape so you may have to examine many masks to find one that fits properly. To test a mask for fit, put it up against you face, being sure there is no hair under the edges, and breathe in through your nose to create a negative air pressure. Air pressure from outside alone should hold the mask in place for a minute or so if the fit is proper.

Today many masks come with a purge valve through which to expel water that inevitably leaks in, but most experts feel theses valves are superfluous and not worth the extra money. You should learn how to clear you mask of water by lifting a lower corner slightly while exhaling air from you nose to push out the water. This is technique that should be learned as park of you most basic snorkeling instruction.

If you normally wear eyeglasses, it is well worth having prescription lenses installed in your facemask. Although it is an added expense, it greatly enhances your underwater viewing and enriches the whole experience.

Snorkel. Extremely basic, a rood snorkel is also extremely simple. It should have a soft, comfortable mouthpiece over which you lips will seal and which your teeth can grip. Beyond the J-turn, the tube should be essentially straight and unencumbered by any valves or other devices.

Fins. Swim fin designs are undergoing a variety of modifications and fins should be purchased from someone who really knows the strengths and weaknesses of various styles for different purposes. The wrong fins can result in tire muscles and severe foot cramps that are both uncomfortable and dangerous. The trend has been to create fins that give greater power. Power fins are less important for most freshwater snorkelers, but for those diving where river currents are strong or there is much tidal surge, power fins can almost be considered a necessity

Underwater Note taking: Since paper disintegrates in water, make underwater journals of the acetate sheets used for overhead projectors. Punch holes in the top left corner of each sheet and join them all with a plastic split ring. Tie the ring with the acetate onto your wrist. Mark with a grease pencil. At home you can either copy these notes into your regular journal or put acetate on a copy machine and print out a hard copy. When done, clean the acetate sheets with a mild degreaser, dry and you are ready for your next underwater outing.

MAPPING EQUIPMENT

Compasses. The core of any good mapping tool kit is a good compass and your knowledge of how to use It.. The range of available compasses is great and somewhat confusing. A full range of quality compasses, along with a top-notch instruction guide, is over by Silva Systems. A reasonably inexpensive but very good general compass, the Silva Explorer III—type 3 is an excellent choice both for direction finding and simple map making. A more sophisticated model, at about three times the price, is the Silva Ranger—Type 15. It has a liquid-filled transparent housing, a sapphire bearing for the needle, luminous points, and a sighting mirror. It is an excellent compass for those who spend much time afield, particularly in wild land. With a good compass, you are set to do sound basic mapping and to find your way in unfamiliar countrDistance Measuring Devices. For much of your work laying out transects or quadrats you need a good measuring device. Many people like a measuring tape on a reel. These can usually be had in 50-,100-165-,200-. And 300-foot lengths and many come with English Measurements on one edge and metric units on the other, offering you a choice of systems. For most botanical work, fiberglass tapes area quite accurate, durable enough, and less expensive than steel ones. For laying out transect lines and quadrat boundaries, some people prefer to use a measuring wheel. You roll the wheel from point to point and it records the distance it has been rolled.

SOURCES

A number of items for a botanical tool kit are not commonly found in stores of the average community. Below is a list of addresses of the major catalog companies:

Acorn Naturalists
155 El Camino Real
Tustin, CA 92780

Brookstone Company
Nashua, New Hampshire

Carolina Biological Supply Co
2700 York Road.
Burlington, NC 27215

Powell Laboratories Division
Gladston, Or 97027

Edmund Scientific
101 E. Gloucester Pike
Barrington, NJ 08007

General Supply Corporation
P.O. Box 9347
Jackson, MI 39206

Hach Chemical Company
P.O. Box 389
Loveland, CO 90537

LaMotte Chemical Products Co.
P.O.329

Chestertown, MD 21620

The Nature Gift Store
P.O. Box 1959
Kingston, WA 98346

NASCo
901 Janesville Ave.
Ft. Atkinson, WI 53538

Sudbury Laboratories, Inc (Soil Test Kits)
75 Union Avenue
Sudbury, MA 01776

Wards Natural Science Establishment, Inc.
P.O. Box 92912
Rochester, NY 14692-9012

In this day and age of company buy-outs and changing headquarters you are well advised to look up these companies on the Internet to see if their addresses have changed recently. Most of them now are set up to let you order on-line.

QUADRATS AND TRANSECTS-STUDY TOOLS

Choosing A Study Area

Choice of a study area depends upon several factors: the kind of plant activity you want to explore; the amount and regularity of the time you can devote to your plant interest; and the distance you can afford to travel too carry on your pursuits. The marvelous thing about plant watching is that there are species to be found virtually anywhere you may find yourself, things to be seen close to home and in far corners of the Earth. Writer, naturalist, and philosopher Henry David Thoreau did much plant watching throughout his life, and most of it was done very close to home. To emphasize opportunities of close observations of the near-at-hand, he wrote that he had "traveled widely in Concord."

First observations are probably best made of path-side plants along a route you travel regularly. It is easy to find a few specimens upon which to focus. Follow their fates through the various seasons of the year, noting the phases of their lives and the trials they face. Once you find yourself becoming more deeply involved in the events of plant's lives, you will be ready to move from initial casual observation toward a somewhat more studied and systematic approach.

It should be possible to find an uncultivated patch near home. In the city it may be a vacant lot or park. For the suburbanite it may be a yard, park, or nature center. In such places you may be able to place some marker to identify individuals of species, or plots of habitat that you want to follow more closely. Markers must be subtle so as not to attract the attention of mischief-makers and vandals—for example, press a golf tee flat into the ground. We will explore such marking techniques a bit later.

In addition to near-at-hand sites, which are the best for regular observation throughout several seasons, there are many places you may wish to explore more intensively over shorter periods of time, such as during a vacation period. Such places include state and national forests and parks; community conservation lands, wildlife refuges, habitats protected by the Nature Conservancy; botanical reserves; Audubon sanctuaries, and other similar public and private lands where natural communities are given some degree of permanent protection from development.

If you plan to observe without disturbing the plant life in any way, you will have little difficulty carrying our your goals. However, if you want to manipulate the plants or their environments, you will need to gather permissions and these may not come without a certain degree of hassle, if at all. The hassling can be grossly annoying, but the officials responsible for land cannot be expected to recognize your good intentions immediately, nor are e always sensitive to officialdom's need not to set difficult precedents when dealing with thousands of users of the land.

ESTABLISHING STUDY PLOTS

If you main interests are in following life histories of certain species and keeping phenological records, you will usually need only some well-delineated study plots to which you can return from time to time. On the other hand, if you wish to record plant association and succession you will need to establish those study plots according to the more rigorous sampling procedures discussed later. Even in following life histories and phenological phenomena, be sure to collect data on enough individual species to reflect what is common, not merely what is unique to a few individuals or a localized population In general, the larger the number of individuals you are following and the further apart they are growing, the less likely you are to have the information skewed by anomalies, and the more likely that information is to be reliable for the species as a whole.

Choice of plot size depends upon the species you are planning to observe. Normally, small species require smaller plots than larger species and abundant species require smaller plots than rare species. The following can be used as a rule-of-thumb guide to study plot size:

Mosses, liverworts, and lichens	0.1 square meter
Herbaceous plants and tree seedlings	1.0 square meter
Shrubs and saplings up to ten feet tall	10 to 20 square meters
Large trees	100 square meters

You can use yards and other English units instead of meters, but the metric system is the universal system of scientists and you data will be more widely useful to others if you use the metric system in all your explorations.

MARKING PLOTS

Both in the short and long run, you will want to be able to relocate you study plots easily. If you own the study area, it is easier to put in permanent and reasonably conspicuous study plot boundary markers. Lengths of pipe driven into the corners of the study plot are good durable markers. These should protrude a few inches above the ground, their height depending upon safety considerations to walkers and machinery. When such a study plot is under active observation, wooden or metal stakes a meter or more long can be set inside the pipes to make plot corners more visible, and string can be tied to these stakes to establish boundary lines.

On property you don't own it is more likely that aesthetic and/or vandal consideration will make it impractical to install highly visible corner markers. In such cases, it is more feasible to drive one stake down close to ground level. This should be done consistently in the same corner of each study plot, usually the southwest corner.

When you set up the plot the first time, take a compass reading from the southwestern corner to the northwest corner and measure the appropriate distance between the markers. Nest, measure the appropriate distance to the northeastern marker, which should be located 90 degrees from the line between the two western stakes. With the two side measurements and the compass you can at any time reconstruct any study plot from its single stake and your notes. That base stake should be locatable by distance and azimuth references from permanent landmarks such as distinctive boulders, pathways, or stone walls, A person several decades in the future may want to relocate that study area to see if certain plant or species are still surviving at that particular site and to note such changes as have occurred.

Another type of single stake marking system is useful when you are focusing on one species. That system involves driving a stake in the center of your proposed study plot and conceiving the plot as a large circle rather than a rectangle. Sight each individual plant you plan to study from the central marker and using a compass, string, and/or measuring tape, give and azimuth and dis tance reading from the stake. Again be sure to get a good location fix for the base stake from permanent landmark feature. It is useful to assign each study plot a Roman numeral designation and each individual plant an Arabic numeral. This makes it possible to provide each plant a code name that can be correlated with appropriate data recorded in your journal.

Such central stakes are also useful for setting up tristat points, which are points over which a camera tripod can be accurately set. Photographs are regularly taken in different direction from these points, with the azimuth being duly noted for each shot. A sequence of photos taken through the seasons and over a span of years provides a most useful record of seasonal and successional changes in vegetation. Such records are all too few yet are relatively easily gathered by anyone with interest, concern, and dedication. If locations of tristat markers are filed with a local plant society, others can follow up what you started if you move to a new location or become incapacitated in some way.

Rather than using study plots per se some people merely focus on certain individuals or clumps of plants of a given species that they find along a route they regularly travel. The location of these should be carefully noted so that they can be checked in other years or by other people. This can be done by mapping the route, usually in a sequence of short lengths between permanent landmarks. The numbers on utility poles are useful along roads and transmission lines. Within each of these segments of the route note the distance from the landmark to the plant at right angles to the route of travel. Note whether the plant is to the right or left of the route and roughly estimate its distance from either the center or the edge of the path, (be sure to indicate which each time). The accuracy of your measurements will depend upon the species and the terrain. Your normal walking pace is usually a sufficient measuring device, but you may wish to be more accurate for some purposes and utilize a measuring tape. Taking such measurements is time-consuming and something of a nuisance, but it often proves invaluable in trying to relocate a plant a year or so later after a dormant period.

LESS IS ENOUGH

The ambitious beginner may want to investigate every plant in an area. Even when concentrating on a single species, particularly if it is a common species, it does not take long to realize that ambition must be curbed by reality. Just as you cannot know the details of the lives of all your human neighbors, you cannot know all your plant neighbors either. You have to concentrate on a few species in a few communities, and even then you have to sample the population.. And there's the rub. How do you go about determining what is an adequate sample to provide information that is reasonably reliable and valid? You must turn to the science of professional gamblers, the tools of determining the odds that given events will or will not occur—in short *statistics*.

It is not within the realm of this book to elaborate on statistics, but it is instructive to look at some basic strategies for sampling the vegetation. Such strategies are not unduly threatening, yet they will increase the value of the information gathered while indulging in the joy of plant exploration In essence, you will use the same procedures presented in the section on study plots but give the plots fancier names and determine how many such plots to use in a study area and of what size and distribution. It really is not so difficult as might be feared.

USING QUADRATS FOR SAMPLING

When you set about asking and answering quantitative quest such as how many individual of a species are found in a particular plant community, or how much space in a community is occupied by a particular species, or how widely the species is distributed throughout a community, you will find it profitable to sample the study area by using a number of standardized study plots known as *quadrats*. These are simply plots of the same size and shape distributed in one of several appropriate patterns through the vegetation. Because of their identical form for any given study, information gathered from quadrats can be compared and used to project with a significant degree of accuracy concepts about more of the plant life of that community. Of course that information can never be as accurate as when every plant is examined. None-the-less it can be quite accurate with a greatly reduced amount of time and effort.

For many studies, qualitative information is enough. You can determine whether a species is abundant, common, or rare, but usually we need to know just how abundant, how common, and how rare. It is important to set some base-line information to determine what trends indicate a continuing decline, it is often essential to begin work to prevent further decline of a species whit it still is more abundant than rare. On the other hand, some species seem always to have been rare, and their numbers today do not indicate any significant decline. Such data are gathered through ongoing studies using quadrat-sampling methods. It is very easy to be fooled when making qualitative analysis of the plants around you, for some species stand out because of size, shape, or color. Other species that may be even more abundant are often hidden in the surrounding foliage or have less conspicuous features. Quantitative sampling makes the data much more objective.

Although the word quadrat derives from the Latin for "squared", quadrats are not necessarily square. They can be rectangular, or even circular. In any given study, the key is that all quadrates will be of comparable shape and area. Actual choice of shape depends upon the nature of the vegetation to be explored, while the number and area of quadrats to be used at a particular study area depends upon the number of species in the study area and their density

Circular plots, or *circlats*, can be used most effectively in areas of low vegetation such as grasses, bryophytes, lichens, and such. These circlat plots tend to give more valid results than a similar number of square plots in the same area. Circular plots are easy to lay out because you need only a stake, some marker pegs, and a length of cord attached to a ring that will fit loosely over the stake. First determine the area that you must enclose (see Species/area curves below) and calculate the proper radius for such a circle. Mark this on your string measuring from the ring. Slip the ring over the stake that is driven in the center of what is to be your circlat. Then move the taut string around, putting a marker peg in the ground at useful intervals. Pull out the center stake and move to the next place you want a circlat and repeat the process. Or, for more permanent circlats, you can leave the center stake in p lace, removing the circumferential markers. For short-term studies in which you are not concerned about relocating the exact site of the quadrat, you can make up portable circlat hoops. Cut lengths of light hose equal to the circumference of your plat. Snugly insert a wooden dowel into one end of the hose section and bend the section into a circle, slipping the dowel into the other end. You can further divide this into pie-shaped sectors by tying strings across the diameter of the hoop. This is particularly useful if you have some friends to help you with counts in the field. Divide your group into teams of as many sectors as you have put in your hoop—usually two or four. Each team member censuses one sector of the hoop quadrat.

Square and rectangular quadrats can be used with vegetation of any height. The square format is the most limited because it is least likely to encompass variety in an area, particularly if there appears to be any sort of environmental gradient in operation. The square format seems most appropriate in highly uniform vegetation where species diversity is limited. This does not mean that square quadrats cannot be used elsewhere only that the results are apt to be less accurate than if rectangular-shaped plots are employed. With their greater length than width for the same area they are more likely to detect variations. If a gradient of some sort is perceived, such as moisture, soil texture, or shading, orient the rectangle with its long axis parallel to the gradient

We now need to explore a basic technique for reasonably determining an appropriate size and number of sampling plots to use in any of your studies. What we seek is a balance between sample size adequate to provide reasonable information and one in which the work is overwhelming and impractical. Particularly for the amateur, we don't want the work to be so great that it ceases to be fun or creates a chore far larger than that to which we can devote available time.

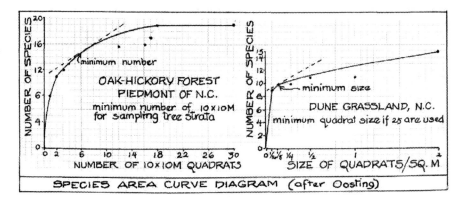

Figure D-4

SPECIES/AREA CURVES

In the section on simple study areas, some rough plot sizes for different sizes of vegetation were listed. These sizes were assembled from some simple averages for that type of vegetation by using a mathematical technique, species/ area curves, from data on a variety of habitats. These suggested plot sizes are probably adequate for the initial studies of most serious plant observers. A bit more difficult is determining how many such plots are needed for accurate data. Both figures can be determined by minor variants of a species/curve analysis.

The process involves doing some sapling in the habitat and plotting a graph of the data. The data involved are the number of different species found and either the number of standard plots used of the size of the nested quadrats examined (see page x). The number of species is plotted on the vertical axis of the graph and the number or size of the quadrat is plotted on the horizontal axis. Each of the data points is then roughly connected by a line to form a distinctive curve.

The curve will normally rise quickly to some point; then further increase in number or size will yield smaller increases in the number of addition species added to the total so that the curve will flatten. This simply means that it takes an increasingly greater amount of effort to get less and less additional information. The question is, when is enough enough? After the curve begins to break from its rise, we start to ask how much the information we seek is worth the extra effort to get it. There is nor pat answer, but most agree that it is somewhere beyond the break in the curve. A frequent standard has been that point where a ten—percent increase in number of plots or area of plots results in an increase in species of no more than ten percent of the total number of species.

Shape of the curves will vary, so determining that point on your graph is not possible simply by eyeballing; you will have to do a little additional drawing on your graph. First locate that point on the graph where ten percent of the number of total species occurs and move over to intersect the point that represents ten percent of the number of plots sampled or area sampled. Mark the point and then draw a line through it and the zero point on the axis. Next draw a line parallel to the one just drawn but such that it is tangent to the species area curve. Mark the point of tangency. The point directly below it on the horizontal axis will indicate the minimum number of plots, or sizes of plots that should be used for reasonably accurate information.

PLACING THE QUADRATS

Once you have determined appropriate size and number of quadrats, there
remains the question of how should these be distribute in the study area so
that they most truly representing conditions of the stand as a whole. The need
is to avoid personal preconception of what is typical of the area, thus, perhaps
unwittingly, putting a bias to the data. If an area were truly uniform in distribution of plant species, there would be no problem. Each quadrat would
equally represent the whole stand. But such does not occur in the real world.
Therefore, the study areas are imagined to be divided into a large number of
plots each the size of your quadrats and each representing a segment of the
whole. The name of the game is to choose the selection of the plots so randomly that each has an equal chance of being chosen whenever a selection is
made The basic assumption of the statistical analysis is that no valid conclusion can b drawn unless the samples have been taken at random.

Setting up random selection of plots, free of human error, is not easy. Perhaps the simplest way is to run a grid-line lottery. Map the whole study area
and then overlay it with a grid. Number the horizontal lines and letter the vertical lines of the grid. Cut a number of slips of paper and a grid line number or
letter on each slip. Place all the letters of the vertical grid lines in one container
and the horizontal grid lines in another. Shake up the containers thoroughly
and then beg in your lottery. Draw one slip from each container, and then
place a sample plot where the intersecting lines designated by each slip occur.
Repeat this process until you have drawn an appropriate number of plot place-
ments.

The resultant distribution of quadrats may appear inappropriate, with some
areas heavily sampled and others neglected. Such are the whims of random
chance. The fewer the number of quadrats being used, the more likely it is that
such skewed distributions will occur. The larger the number of plots, the more
the pattern appears to be even-handed.

Statistical analysis is not always of help in studying a given problem such as
how plants are distributed along a particular gradient. In such situations systematic placing of plots is often preferable. To do this simply, mark of a base
line of arbitrary length. At uniform intervals along the base line run perpendicular lines. Use a compass to determine direction and pace off equal intervals
along each perpendicular and establish the quadrats. Keep to you line and distance. It biases the data to shift the quadrat a bit in some direction to include
plants that intrigue you but that would be excluded by sticking to the rule.

If you are carefully sampling a plant community that has several well-defined layers, you may wish to use nested quadrats to deal with each of the different layers. Starting in one corner, build ever-larger squares from your smallest area to your largest (see Figure x) Nested blocks can also be used in determining quadrat sizes with in a species/area curve. Be sure to separately the data for each sub-block as well as including it in the data of the larger block.

As you can now see readily, setting up quadrats properly can be rather time-consuming but results gathered using this method are generally good.

LINE TRANSECTS

Another sampling technique can be used to gather much of the same data; it is somewhat more rapid and more objective to use *this line transect method*. It involves running several lines through a plant community and then identifying, counting, or measuring all plants that touch, underlie, or overhang the transect line. Transects are particularly useful in open areas such as grassland, marshes, and shrublands. They are less appropriate in tree lands. Useful for exploring environmental gradients, succession and the zones between two habitats (*ecotones*) line transects are much more practical than quadrats in dense, brushy vegetation. A line transect can be used to calculate species abundance and frequency, although not with quite the same accuracy as with a quadrat. Density per se cannot be calculated by this method, but you can calculate relative density.

In any given study, all of the transect lines should be of equal length. For some studies you will want to sample randomly. Ro do this, mark a stick at one end, take it in you hand, close your eyes, spin around several times, and then toss the stick. Lay out your lines in the direction toward which the stick points, beginning at the marked end of the stick. On the other hand, successional and environmental gradient studies will best be studied using a uniform spacing system the runs parallel to the expected gradient. Sample size normally ranges between twenty—five and thirty transect lines. This demands time, but not as much as a quadrat study.

For sampling such things as frequency of occurrence, you will want to have your transect line marked at equal intervals. This can be achieved most simply by using a cloth measuring tape as your transect line. But you can also carry a cord that has been knotted at equal intervals or marked with paint or ink. A reasonable length for mot transects is twenty to thirty meters (100 ft tape) The line will be shorter for some transition areas and longer for others; it depend on the nature of the plant transition zones you are investigating.

BELT TRANSECTS

A belt transect is essentially a line of square quadrats laid end to end. In one sense it is a wide transect line, in another it is an extra-long, rectangular quadrat. The belt transect effectively combines some of the best qualities of quadrats and transects and compensates for some of the weaknesses of each. Belt transects are most useful in studying subtle abiotic gradients and successional changes.

Belt transects should normally be twenty to thirty times as long as wide. Thus, a one-meter wide strip for studying herbaceous plants would be about thirty meters long, while a 0.1-meter wide strip for studying bryophyte communities would be about three meters long. As a rule you should lay out enough belt transects to cover ten percent of the study area. Because you would generally use this method when exploring abiotic gradients, you should lay out the belts in a systematic pattern that runs parallel to the apparent direction of gradation.

For a couple of reasons it is useful to section off the belt into square quadrats First, you can perhaps get helpers to collect data on the separate units and thus reduce the individual workload and increase the sociability of your field work. Second, if the belt is quite long and the gradients quite gradual you can collect data from alternate squares. If y o do this, be sure to be consistent. If you do it on one belt, you must do the same for all belts in that study.

There are other variants of the quadrat and transect sampling techniques that have special statistical traits appropriate to certain types of studies. However, the ones present her should sever most needs until you have grown beyond the sophistication of this book. By then you will have discovered professional friends who can guide you through their intricacies.

THE BISECT

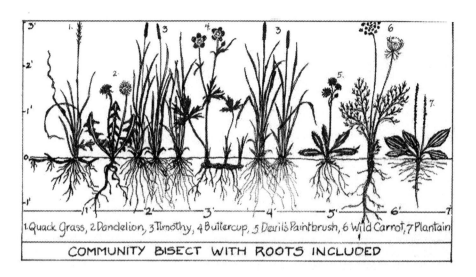

1.Quack Grass, 2.Dandelion, 3.Timothy, 4.Buttercup, 5.Devils Paintbrush, 6.Wild Carrot,7.Plantain

COMMUNITY BISECT WITH ROOTS INCLUDED

Figure D-5

Quadrats and transects have a basically two-dimensional bias. Vegetation, however is three-dimensional. The eager field observer may wish to build a picture or a vertical cross section of a study area. This is known as a *bisect*. Some bisect are prepared showing just the vegetation from ground to canopy. These are comparatively easy to prepare, but a complete bisect indicates the depth and distribution of the roots and other underground parts. It involves digging a ditch and thus is time-consuming and difficult work.

Preparing a bisect involves drawing the vegetation to scale on graph paper and indicating the proper height and lateral reach of each individual. Use a letter code to indicate the species represented. When possible, the bisect will also indicate the depth and lateral spread of the roots of the species in the plane of the bisect.

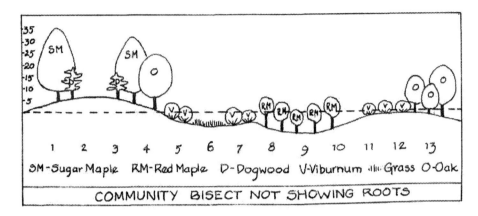

Figure D6

-Figures D5 and D6 illustrate bisects of two different kinds of communities.

WHAT INFORMATION TO GATHER

Now that you know about the mechanics or quadrats and transects, what kind of information should you gather with their aid? Actually, there is a wide variety of information that can be pursued. Depending upon your interest you may want to, or indeed be able to, pursue only a few of them at any given time. Of course, having gone to the effort of setting up a system of quadrats, it makes sense to mine it for as much information as possible.

Species lists. Among the most basic data are listings of species present in each quadrat or along a transect. This information helps you understand the diversity in the community and provides data for determining an index of similarity between two communities.

Frequency measures the percent of the total number of samples that contain representatives of a particular species. It is calculated so:

<u>Number of quadrats in which the species occurs</u> x100=Frequency
    Total number of quadrats

What does it mean "to be present" in a quadrat? Some people count only plants rooted within the plot; others count a species present if its shoots or leaves enter the quadrat. Whichever method you follow should be duly entered into your notes as either" rooted frequency" or "shoot frequency". Frequency provides clues to the importance of a species in a community. The higher the frequency the greater its importance. Of even greater use in determining a particular species' importance is relative frequency—that is, comparison of a species' frequency to total frequency of all species present. Calculate thus:

Frequency of a species x 100=Relative frequency
Total frequency of all species

Abundance. Although often stated in qualitative terms, such as rare or common, abundance can be stated more quantitatively by comparing the number of individual of a species with the total number of individuals of all species. This is usually stated as a percentage and is calculated thusly:

Number of the given species x 100=Abundance
Total number of all species

A high abundance figure does not necessarily reflect a high importance for the species in the community since larger species, whose shade strongly influences the community, may be far less abundant than smaller species that carpet the ground.

Density. Density is of more importance than abundance for determining the significance of a species in the community. It is a measure of the number of individuals of a particular species per unit of area. Thus, we need to count all the plants of a particular species from all the quadrats; the total area of all the quadrats then divides this number.

Number of plants of a species =Density
Total area sampled

For example, if I sample twenty 1-meter quadrats and count a total of 250 plants of Canada mayflower, I can say that on average the density of this plant is 12.5 plants for each square meter of the study area.

Cover. Frequency and density of a species are important, but equally important is how much space the plants occupy (cover). It is very difficult to plant a plant's three-dimensional space occupancy but much easier to collect data on the area they cover as perceived from directly above. This is important because shading, which strongly involves mapping each quadrat for the area covered by each plant; the area of the leaf crown for herbaceous and woody plants; the diameter of the root crown for grasses and ferns(with some arching species it will extend beyond the root crown); and, for bryophytes, the area of the plant cluster.

A method used to record cover accurately involves laying a grid over the quadrat that represents squares on a sheet of graph paper. The observer then fills in the portion of each square on the graph paper that represents the corresponding square on the quadrat gid. This is the same technique some artists use to enlarge or reduce drawings. Use a letter code inside each crown area drawn to indicate the species.

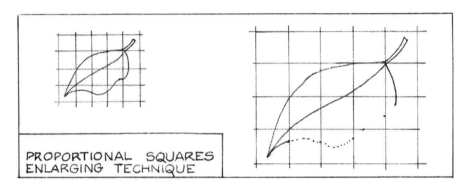

Figure D-5

Once you have crown outlines and an overlay grid, add up all the number of grid squares enclosed by a species. If half or less of a grid square is covered, ignore it; if more than half a grid square is covered include it in your count. Multiply the resulting number by the area of an individual grid square to get the total area occupied by a species. Divide that by the total area of the quadrat. Thus:

Area covered by a specific species x 100=Percent cover
    Area of quadrat

Cover information is useful because it gives a good indication of the dominance of each species in a community. Actually the area of the quadrat may not always be the most useful divisor for the formula because the whole area may not be totally covered with vegetation, particularly in unproductive environments. More appropriate is the total cover by all species. This gives as a result a measure of relative cover.

Importance Value. To get an indication of the importance of a particular species in a community, sum up the three values of relative frequency, relative density, and relative cover.

Abiotic Data. Data on such abiotic factors as temperature, light, soil texture, and soil structure should be gathered for each plot. It can later be correlated with plant information.

Zoological Data. In some studies you will also want to collect data on the animal life present in the quadrats, particularly those species that feed on the plants or are important for pollination or seed dispersal.

WHAT CAN YOU LEARN?

Setting up formal study plots such as quadrats, transects, circlats, and bisects takes considerable effort. It is certainly much easier to ramble through glade and wood enjoying the beauty of many species or the thrill of discovery of the occasional station of a rare species. If, however, you are truly curious, you will want to understand what is happening in the life history of particular species or what goes on in a plant community over a period of time. When compelled by such curiosity, you will find joy and excitement in the work of setting up the formal study plots and examining them intently.

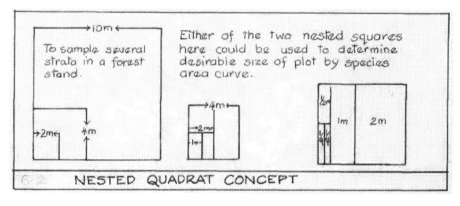

Figure D-6

Study plots help focus your purely qualitative observations. You get some very interesting information from them regarding species' life histories and phenology. Using the various vegetative sampling techniques you can gather information that:

1. allows comparison of two or more plant communities.

2. reveals changes occurring within a community over time.

3. Permits correlation of variation in vegetation with variation in zoological and abiotic factors.

Your next step is to get help with basic statistical techniques to manipulate data properly so that they will reveal the degree of comparison or correlation and the degree of significance of the calculations. Some data can be presented effectively in graphic form, which allows visual comparison. Other data h as to be processed through a spate of mathematical formulas resulting in abstract mathematical expression. Many professional field biologists are themselves poor manipulators of the data, but they team up with statisticians who help them design appropriate manipulation and thus determine the kind of data that will have to be gathered. The also get the statistician to help them process the data. A serious amateur nee feel no embarrassment in seeking help with statistical design and data manipulation.

OUTDOOR MANNERS FOR THE PLANT OBSERVER

All outdoors-people must learn to exhibit good outdoor manners if they are to be welcome afield by both Nature and other people. Increasingly outdoor recreationists have been unmannerly and have stimulate a spate of No Trespassing signs and unfriendly attitudes among landowner. Those with poor outdoor manners stress the natural systems and the goodwill of thoughtful people. *No group of outdoor users is without its slobs; let's not count you among them.*

- **If you pack it in, pack it out, whether on land or at sea. Leave no debris from eating, photography, and the like. Also, go the extra mile. When you find someone else's thoughtless refuse, pack it out too.**

- Always seek permission to use private lands. A thank-you note never huts either.

- If you use gates, be sure they are securely latched behind you.

- Always walk the edge of tilled fields. Never walk through crops or hay.

- Do not park vehicles so that they bloc the passage of others.

- If you use trail bikes or other motorized, rough-terrain vehicles to gain access to wild land, choose routes very carefully to minimize erosion and destruction of vegetation. Avoid all ecologically fragile lands such as dunes, tundra, vernal pools, and most desert sites.

- Never collect living plant material without the landowner's prior permission.

- Keep collecting to the barest minimum—take only voucher specimens and then only when identification is questionable. If there are flower pickers in you party, urge them to observe the rule of ten; that is, pick one only if you can see ten other from that point.

- Just because plants don't run away, don't be unduly noisy and frighten away wildlife that others may want to observe.

• Keep markers for quadrats and other study devices inconspicuous and unobtrusive so as not to intrude unduly on the aesthetic experiences of others.

• *Particularly in back country, leave a rough itinerary of your travels, along with expected time of return with a responsible person who will then know where to look for you if you are detained.*

APPENDIX F—FURTHER READING

Bookstores carry a limited stock of nature books and public libraries often have only a very limited shelf-list of botanical titles. Consequently, interested amateurs are often unaware of the many botanical titles that have been published over the years. The purpose of this list is to broaden awareness of the existence of some books that may prove interesting and enlightening to the amateur plant observer.

When a title is not available at your local library, ask the librarian to try and get for you through an interlibrary loan. Check with Amazon.com to see if the book is available from them either new or used. Many of the books are quite expensive (in the $100 range) so it will be to your advantage to get them through some form of library cooperation. You can also look in used book stores for titles that are no longer in print. College and university libraries are more likely to have some of these books than are public libraries, but even there you may have to check botany department libraries or even the personal libraries of cooperative professors. Be persistent in your searching.

GENERAL

Ayensu, Heywood. Lucas and DeFillipps, *Our Green and Living World: The Wisdom To Save It,* Smithsonian Institution, 1984

Corner, E.J. H., *The Life of Plants.* World Publishing Co. 1964 Felt, E.P., *Plant Galls and Gall Makers,* Comstock Publishing Co. 1940

Graham L., Graham J., Wilcox L.W. and Graham, J., *Plant Biology* Prentice-Hall 2002

Harlow, William M., *The Unseen World of Plants: Patterns of Life,* Harper& Row, 1966

Harris, Marjorie, *Botanica North America: An Illustrated Guide to Native Plants* Harper Resources, 2003

Moore, David M., *Our Green Planet—The Story of Plant Life on Earth* Cambridge University Press, 1982

Palmer and Fowler, *Fieldbook of Natural History,* McGraw-Hill, 1975 Podolsky, Alexander S. New Phenology. John Wiley & Sons, 1984 Salisbury, Frank B., *The Biology of Flowering,* Natural History Press, 1971 Schwartz. Mark D. and Mark Donald Schwartz. *Phenology: An Integrative Environmental Science.* Kluwer Academic Publishers, 2004 Thompkins, Peter and Christopher Bird, *The Secret Lives of Plants,*

Harper & Row, 1973

Wilson, Ron, *How Plants Grow.* Larousse and Co. 1980

PLANT ECOLOGY AND GEOGRAPHY

Andrews, W. A. *A Guide to the Study of Soil Ecology,* Prentice-Hall, 1973

Bazzaz, F.A. *Plants in Changing Environments: Linking Physiological, Population and Community Ecology,* Cambridge University Press, 1996

Crawley, Michael, *Plant Ecology,* Blackwell Science, 1996

Eastman, John, *The Book of the Forest and Thicket,* Stackpole Books, 1992

Grieg-Smith, P. *Quantitative Plant Ecology. 3rd Edition,* University of California Press, 1983

Grime, S.A. *Plant Strategies, Vegetative Strategies, and Ecosystem Properties 2nd edition,* John Wiley and Sons, 2001

Gurevitch, Jessica, Samuel Scheineur, Gordon Fox, *The Ecology of Plants,* Sinauer Associates, 2002

Jorgenson, Neil, A *Sierra Club Naturalists Guide to Southern New England* Sierra Club Books, 1978

Oosting, Henry J. *The Study of Plant Communities,* W.H. Freeman & Company Publishers, 1956

Silvertown, Jonathan W. and Deborah Charlesworth, *Introduction to Plan t Population Biology, 4th edition,* Blackwell Science, 2001

Watt, May Thielgaard, *Reading the Landscape of America,* Collier Books, 1975

HERBACEOUS FLOWERING PLANTS

Baird, Viola Brainerd, *Wild Violets of North America.* University of California Press, 1942

Brown, Lauren, *Weeds in Winter,* W.W. Norton & Company, Inc., 1976

Copeland, L and M. McDonald, *Principles of Seed Science and Technology* Kluwer Academic Publishers, 2001

Elliot, Douglas B. *Roots—An Undergound Botany and Foragers Guide,* Chatham Press, 1976

Kingsley, R. Stern. *Introductory Plant Biology, 9th edition,* McGraw-Hill, 2003

Martin, A and W. Barkley. *Seed Identification Manual* University of California Press, 1961

Poling, James. *Leaves: Their Amazing Lives and Strange Behavior.* Holt, Rinehart and Winston, 1971

Scwartz, Mark D., *Phenology: An Integrative Environmental Science (Tasks for Vegetative Science)* Kluwer Academic Publishers, 2004

TREES AND SHRUBS

Core and Ammons *Woody Plants in Winter.* Boxwood Press, 1958

Forest Service, *Woody—Plant Seed Manual,* U. S. Department of Agriculture Misc. Publication No 654, 1948

Fralish, James S. *Taxonomy and Ecology of Woody Plants in North American* Forests, Wiley, 2002

Harlow, William M. *Fruit and Twig Key to Trees and Shrubs.* Dover, 1946

Heinrich, Bernd, *The Trees In My Forest,* Cliff Street Books, 1997

Hora, Bayard. The Oxford Encyclopedia of Trees of the World. Oxford University Press, 1981

Horn, Henry S. *The Adaptive Geometry of Trees: Monographs in Population Biology,* Princeton University Press, 1971

Peattie, Donald Culross. *A Natural History of Trees of Eastern and Central North America,* Houghton-Mifflin, 1950

Peattie, Donald Culross. A *Natural History of Western Trees.* Bonanza Books, 1953

Stokes, Donald W. *The Natural History of Wild Shrubs and Vines,* Harper & Row 1981

Trelease William. *Winter Botany (Trees and Shrubs)* Dover, 1931

AQUATIC PLANTS

Chadde, Steve W. A Great Lakes Wetland Flora, 2nd edition, Pocketflora Press, 2002

Fassett, Norman C. A Manual of Aquatic Plants. University of Wisconsin Press,1957

Haslam, S.M. River Plants. Cambridge University Press, 1978

Magee, Dennis W. Freshwater Wetlands. University of Massachusetts Press, 1981

NONFLOWERING PLANTS

Bland, John H. Forests *of Lilliput: The Realm of Lichens and Mosses.* Prentice-Hall, 1971

Bodenberg, W. Mosses*: A New Approach to Identification of Common Species* Burgess Publishing Company, 1954

Brightman, Frank H. and B.E. Nicholas. *The Oxford Book of Flowerless Plants,* Oxford University Press, 1966

Brode, Irwin B. and Stephen Shamoff, *Lichens of North America,* Yale University Press, 2001

Crum, Howard A. and Lewis E. Anderson. *Mosses of Eastern North America.* 2 volumes, Columbia University Press, 1981

Dawson E.Y. Marine *Botany, an Introduction*, Holt, Rinehart and Winston, 1966

Frankel, Edward. Ferns *: A Natural History*, Stephen Greene, 1981

Purvis, William. Lichens, Smithsonian Books, 2000

Shaw, Jonathan and Bernard Goffinet, *Bryophyte Biology*, Cambridge University Press,2000

Shuttlesworth, F.S. and Herbert Zim, *Nonflowering Plants*, Golden Press, 1967

978-0-595-36644-6
0-595-36644-9

Printed in the United States
96093LV00003B/217-225/A